Cooking with Chardonnay

75 Sensational Chardonnay Recipes

by

Barbara and Norm Ray

Hoffman Press
A division of Rayve Productions

On the cover: Chardonnay grapes

Cover design: Randall F. Ray
Interior illustrations: William J. Geer

Hoffman Press
A division of Rayve Productions Inc.
Box 726, Windsor, CA 95492

Quantity discounts and bulk purchases of this and other Hoffman Press books are available through Rayve Productions Inc. For more information and to place orders call toll-free 1-800-852-4890 or fax 707-838-2220.

Library of Congress Cataloging-in-Publication Data

Ray, Barbara, 1941 -
   Cooking with chardonnay : 75 sensational chardonnay recipes /
   by Barbara and Norm Ray.
      p. cm.
   Includes index.
   ISBN 1-877810-54-1 (alk.paper)
   1. Cookery (Wine) 2. Wine and wine making. I. Ray, Nor. II. Title

TX726.R377 2002
641.6'22--dc21

                                                        2002036605

To Virginia and Bob,

who guided and encouraged us with their

. . . joie de vivre

. . . excellent recipes

and

. . . wise words

Introduction to Chardonnay

Chardonnay is one of the most popular white table wines throughout the world because its unique flavors are ideal for drinking and cooking and many excellent vintages are readily available at reasonable prices. Fine Chardonnays are a taste treat, rich and complex with a depth of flavors and a long, lingering aftertaste. Most Chardonnays can be stored for years, sometimes decades, their subtle flavors, textures, and aromas improving with age.

Chardonnay wines vary widely in flavor, depth, complexity and dryness, which are determined by the source appellation, viticultural area, vintage, winemaking techniques, and numerous other subtle factors. Some Chardonnays have a distinct fruity flavor – peach, pear, fig, lemon, apple, or pineapple; others are charmingly acidic with a heavier texture and oak overtones. A high-quality Chardonnay should be delicious when first released, reach maturity in two to five years, and age well for 10 to 12 years.

The increasing popularity of Chardonnay coincides with our increasing enjoyment of lighter meals that include more salads, fish and poultry. Chardonnay pairs well with these foods and is ideal for use in cooking them. Chardonnay also adds delightful flavors when cooking lean pork, veal, and some red meat recipes. If you enjoy the flavors of a specific Chardonnay, by all means try it in a recipe.

Cooking with Wine Can Be Good
for Your Health

You can reduce the amount of calories, sodium, fat and cholesterol dramatically when you cook with wine. Wine adds a richness to food that easily replaces high calorie ingredients. Using dessert as an example, fruit that is poached in wine and served with a cookie or two has less than half the calories of a slice of chocolate cake.

You may use less salt, too, when you cook with wine. We enjoy the flavor of coarsely ground kosher salt or sea salt, but if you prefer little or no salt, don't use it. Salt can usually be replaced by the flavorful nuances of the ingredients in the dish when combined with wine. You can also greatly reduce the amount of fats and oil that you use very simply. In place of the usual butter, margarine or cooking oil, use a few drops of olive oil or a spritz or two of cooking oil to cook meat, poultry or fish, then use wine liberally to complete the cooking by poaching instead of frying.

When frying foods, you can easily make a sauce that will be a true gourmet's delight ... with fat and calories greatly reduced. Simply combine wine with the brown bits from the pan, and stir in a little flour to thicken the sauce.

Cholesterol levels, too, are greatly decreased and the natural goodness of your dish is enhanced when wine is used in place of cheese, cream, butter and fat.

It's nice to know that it is possible to eat well, drink well, and enjoy better nutrition, too, isn't it?

Cooking-with-Wine Basics

You can't cook well with bad wine. Nothing has ever been found that equals wine in cooking, but you can't cook well with bad wine. If a Chardonnay tastes vinegary, raw or unpleasant, throw it out. A small amount of bad wine can ruin a dish, just as one rotten apple can spoil a barrelful.

Cook with wine you enjoy. The most important guide in choosing a specific Chardonnay for your cooking is your taste buds. It's a good idea to review published wine evaluations and talk with wine experts about various brands of Chardonnay, but, ultimately, you should select a good-quality wine that tastes good to you. If you don't like the taste, don't use it! Cooking will not hide or enhance the flavor; in fact, it will intensify it.

You don't need expensive vintage wine for cooking. It is important to cook with a moderately priced *good-quality* wine, but not necessarily an expensive *great* wine. The rich subtleties of a great wine's bouquets and flavors, which are so enjoyable when sipping, may be lost or greatly diminished when blended with herbs, spices, and other cooking ingredients and subjected to heat. So, use the good-quality Chardonnay for your cooking, and serve the expensive vintage to accompany it.

Add the wine when the recipe calls for it. *When* you add the wine to the other ingredients is crucial. Don't add it too soon, or too late. Wine performs in certain ways under certain conditions. For example, a beef stew will usually call for the wine to be added early in the recipe so it can marinate the meat, blend with other seasonings, and evaporate its alcohol during cooking.

On the other hand, a soup or dessert may require that wine be added just before it is served to provide the whole flavor of the wine, which would be dispelled if cooked.

Add Chardonnay to suit your taste. When adding Chardonnay to your own recipes, begin with the following portions and add more wine as desired.

	<u>Quantity of Chardonnay Wine</u>
Soups	
Cream, Clear	1 teaspoon per portion
Vegetable, Meat	1 teaspoon per portion
Meats	
Beef, Lamb, Veal	¼ cup per pound
Ham, baked	2 cups for basting
Pastas	
Sauce	¼ cup per portion
Poultry	
Chicken, Turkey, roasted	½ cup per pound for basting
Chicken, poached	½ cup per pound for basting
Duck, Game Hen	¼ cup per portion for basting
Seafood	
Fish, broiled, baked, poached	¼ cup per pound
Fish, sautéed	4 tablespoons per pound
Shellfish	¼ cup per pound
Fruits & Vegetables	
Fresh Fruit	1 teaspoon per portion
Cooked Vegetables	1 teaspoon per portion
Salads	1 teaspoon per portion

Most important of all, enjoy yourself! We do, and we hope that you, too, will enjoy preparing the recipes in this book and creating new recipes using Chardonnay wines. Cooking with wine is a joyous adventure!

Barbara and Norm Ray

Serving Wine

Serving wine correctly adds class to any occasion. Following are tips to give you added confidence when serving your guests.

Temperature: Chardonnay and other white wines require chilling. Place them in the refrigerator for two hours before serving. If you need to chill a bottle of wine quickly, place it in the freezer for 35 minutes. After opening the wine, if it's warm in the room, place the bottle half submerged in a bucket of ice to keep it well chilled.

Wine glasses: Chardonnay tastes better in a tulip-shaped stemmed wine glass with a minimum capacity of 8-10 ounces. The glass should be clear to allow guests to examine the wine's color and body, and it should curve in at the top to retain the wine's bouquet. Hold the glass by the stem to prevent heat from your hand warming the wine.

Pouring wine: Chardonnay should be poured towards the center of the glass. To prevent drips, twist the bottle slightly as you tilt it upright. Fill the glass about two-thirds full, allowing room to swirl the wine and smell its bouquet. At a dinner party, serve wine to women and older guests first, then to men, and, finally, fill your own glass.

FRONT LABEL

1. *Our Own Brand*

2. *1997*

3. *Reserve*

4. *Estate Bottled*

5. *Our Own Vineyard*

6. *The American Valley*

7. **Chardonnay**

8. *Net contents 750ml 13.5% alcohol*

9. *Vinted & bottled by Our Own Winery Wineland, WV, USA*

BACK LABEL

Vinted and Bottled by Our Own Winery, Wineland, WV, USA

10. Government warning: (1) According to the Surgeon General, women should not drink alcoholic beverages during pregnancy due to the risk of birth defects. (2) Consumption of alcoholic beverages impairs your ability to drive a car or operate machinery and may cause health problems. Contains sulfites.

11. The grapes for this wine were grown in our vineyards and vinted in our own winery by members of the same family that planted the original grape vines in 1835. We hope that you will enjoy this wine as much as we did in making it for you.

The Label on the Bottle

A wine bottle label, by law, must provide an accurate description of the wine. That is mandatory. But there is usually a great deal more on the label than that. Here is a guide to reading and understanding terms you'll find on wine bottle labels.

1. The brand name. These days one winery may produce multiple varieties of wines under different labels. Some are secondary lines of wines ... not necessarily inferior, but possibly with less aging, or tank fermented instead of barrel fermented, etc. Other labels may represent a new wine available only in limited quantities.

2. The date. If there is a date on the bottle, it refers to the year the grapes were harvested and the wine made from those grapes, not simply the year in which the wine was made. In the United States, the wine label may list the vintage year if 95 percent of the wine comes from grapes crushed that year.

3. Reserve. This is a term used, by choice, by some vintners to indicate something special about the wine. It may be great grapes, quality barrel aging, or other unique feature.

4. Estate bottled. This term came from France where wineries were traditionally located where the vineyards were. In the United States, where many vineyards are miles away from the winery, "Estate Bottled" indicates that the winery either owns or controls the vineyard and is responsible for the growing of the grapes used in this bottle of wine.

5. The vineyard name. The vineyard name on a wine bottle label indicates that very high-quality grapes were used in the making of that wine. Vineyard designation is purely voluntary on the part of the winery.

6. The appellation. This is a legally protected name under which a wine may be sold, indicating that the grapes used are of a specific kind and are grown in a specific geographic area. By law, 85% of the grapes used in the production of the wine must come from that region.

7. The name of the wine. The wine name may be 1) a grape varietal, such as Chardonnay, Merlot, etc., 2) the name given by the winery to a specific blend of wines, such as Meritage, or 3) a simple proprietary name such as "Red Table Wine."

8. The size of the bottle and the alcohol content. The standard wine bottle is 750 ml. (25.4 oz.), a half bottle is 375 ml., and a split, or one-quarter bottle, is 187 ml. By law, American wines may not contain more than 14% alcohol by volume.

9. The name and address of the bottler.

10. Contains sulfites. Most wines contain sulphur dioxide, a preservative that is added to the wine. Listing all additives on the label is a legal requirement.

11. The message. Many wineries use back labels, too. Here you'll often find useful information about the wine, what flavors it embodies, foods it will pair well with, and other useful facts. Read the back label. It will be helpful in choosing the right wine for the right meal at the right price.

Contents

Seafood

Desserts

Soups

Carrot-Chardonnay Soup

2   **large onions, sliced**
3   **cloves garlic, minced**
2   **shallots, minced**
4   **tablespoons butter**
12 **carrots, peeled and chopped**
4   **cups Chardonnay wine**
2   **cups water**
1   **inch fresh ginger, minced**
2   **sprigs fresh rosemary (3 to 4 inches)**
     Honey to taste
     Salt and pepper
1   **cup whipping cream**

GARNISH:
½   **cup whipping cream**
¼   **teaspoon nutmeg**

Sauté onions, garlic and shallots in butter until limp and translucent. Add carrots and coat with butter. Let cook for just a few minutes. Add the wine and water. Add the minced ginger and rosemary. Simmer until carrots are very tender. Purée vegetables until smooth. Return to pan with cooking liquids.

Adjust seasoning with honey, salt and pepper. Add cream a little at a time. Reheat on low heat. It will round out and smooth the flavors. To garnish, whip the ½-cup whipping cream and set aside. Fold the nutmeg into the cream and mix well. Float dollops of cream on top of soup.

Serves 6

Serve with Chardonnay.

Pea Soup with Wine

½   **pound bacon, finely chopped**
2   **large onions, chopped**
3   **large carrots, thinly sliced**
2   **large potatoes, diced**
1   **cup green split peas, uncooked**
4   **cups water**
2   **cups Chardonnay wine**
1   **ham hock**
1   **bay leaf**
½   **teaspoon black pepper, coarsely ground**
    Sea salt or kosher salt
2   **tablespoons sherry**
    Croutons

In a large kettle, sauté bacon until cooked, but not crisp. Set bacon aside. Add onions and sauté until limp. Add the carrots, potatoes, peas, water, Chardonnay wine, ham hock, bay leaf and pepper. Cover and simmer for 2 hours, stirring often.

Remove ham hock and set aside. Remove bay leaf and discard. Put soup through a sieve, or process in a blender until smooth. Cut the lean ham from the ham hock into small pieces. Return bacon and ham pieces to soup mixture.

Reheat and adjust seasonings; add sherry. Float croutons on top of each serving.

Serves 6 to 8

Serve with Chardonnay.

Maritata, The Italian Marriage Soup

¼   **pound unsalted butter**
1   **cup freshly grated Asiago or Parmesan cheese**
3   **egg yolks**
1   **cup heavy cream**
1   **cup Chardonnay wine**
4   **cups chicken stock**
¼   **pound angel hair or fideo pasta**
    Sea salt or kosher salt to taste
    Freshly ground black pepper
    Chopped parsley or chives for garnish

Cream butter in a food processor. Add grated cheese and process for 2 minutes. Add egg yolks, 1 at a time, processing briefly after each addition.

With the processor running, slowly add cream through feed-tube. Scrape sides of bowl and process again.

Meanwhile, bring Chardonnay wine and chicken stock to a boil in a soup pot. Break pasta into pieces and drop into pot. Cook 8 minutes, or until pasta is al dente. Add some of the hot stock to the mixture in the food processor and process. Pour contents of processor into soup pot, bring to a simmer and season with salt and pepper to taste. Serve immediately, garnished with the parsley or chives.

Serves 4 to 6

Serve with Chardonnay.

5

Cream of Mushroom, Onion and Garlic Soup

¼	pound butter
1	large yellow onion, diced
3	cloves garlic, minced
1½	pounds mushrooms, chopped, divided in half
1	pint chicken stock
2	tablespoons lemon juice
1	pint milk
½	teaspoon thyme
1	bay leaf
½	teaspoon chicken base or bouillon cube
¾	cup flour
2	tablespoons Chardonnay wine
1	pint heavy cream or half and half
	Sea salt or kosher salt and black pepper
	Sliced green onions for garnish

In a large saucepan, melt 1 ounce butter and sauté onion until translucent. Add garlic and half the mushrooms; sauté briefly. Add chicken stock, milk, lemon juice, thyme, bay leaf and chicken base. Heat to a simmer.

In a small saucepan, melt remaining butter and stir in flour to make a roux (smooth paste); cook 5 minutes. Add Chardonnay to mushroom mixture in large saucepan; stir. Blend in roux; simmer 15 minutes more. Add remaining mushrooms. Remove from heat and add cream. Adjust seasoning to taste. Stir thoroughly and garnish with green onions.

Serves 8 to 10

Serve with Chardonnay.

Onion-Mushroom Soup

The flavor of this soup will be enhanced if the onions are cooked slowly.

4	tablespoons butter
6	medium onions, peeled and finely sliced
1	cup fresh mushrooms, chopped
½	teaspoon sea salt or kosher salt
¼	teaspoon black pepper
1	tablespoon flour
2	cups Chardonnay wine
7	cups chicken broth or stock
¼	cup freshly grated Parmesan cheese

Melt the butter in a soup pot. Add the onions. Stir, cover and simmer for 20 minutes, stirring occasionally. Add mushrooms, salt, pepper, flour and wine. Bring to a boil, stirring. Add the broth and simmer, uncovered, for 40 minutes. Serve sprinkled with Parmesan cheese.

Serves 6

Delicious with Chardonnay.

Zesty Cream of Carrot Soup

¼	cup olive oil
1	large onion, diced
1	clove garlic, minced
2	14½-ounce cans chicken broth
½	cup Chardonnay wine
1	pound peeled baby carrots
1	4-ounce can mild green chili peppers, diced
1	teaspoon chili powder
½	teaspoon ground cumin
1	teaspoon sea salt or kosher salt
½	teaspoon black pepper
1	cup half and half
¾	cup sour cream for garnish
	Paprika

In a large saucepan, sauté onion and garlic in hot olive oil. Add chicken broth, Chardonnay wine, carrots, chili peppers, chili powder, cumin, salt and pepper. Bring to boil, reduce heat and simmer, covered, for 10 to 12 minutes, until carrots are very tender.

In a food processor or blender container, process half the soup mixture until smooth. Repeat with remaining mixture. Return all to saucepan. Stir in half and half. Heat through.

Garnish with dollops of sour cream sprinkled with paprika.

Serves 8

Serve with Chardonnay.

Green Chardonnay Soup

4   cups chicken stock
8   (or 1 bunch) whole scallions, trimmed and finely chopped; reserve ½ cup for garnish
1   bunch of watercress, washed and chopped
½   pound fresh spinach, washed, stems removed and chopped
¼   cup fresh chopped parsley
1   cup Chardonnay wine
1   teaspoon sea salt or kosher salt
½   teaspoon ground black pepper
3   egg yolks
¾   cup heavy cream; reserve ¼ cup for garnish
1   teaspoon lemon juice

In a large cooking pan, bring the chicken stock to a boil. Add chopped vegetables, parsley and Chardonnay. Season with salt and pepper. Reduce heat and simmer for 15 to 20 minutes. Purée in a blender or food processor. Return soup to pan and reheat.

Mix egg yolks with ½ cup cream, stir in a little of the hot soup and add this mixture to remaining soup. Heat gently, stirring, until soup thickens slightly. **NOTE:** Do not boil.

Garnish individual servings of soup with a bit of cream and chopped scallions.

Serves 4 to 6

Serve with Chardonnay.

9

Shrimp Bisque

10	tablespoons butter
1	small onion, finely chopped
1	clove garlic, minced
1	small carrot, finely chopped
1	teaspoon dried dill
½	teaspoon dried tarragon
2	pounds medium shrimp, peeled and deveined
1	cup Chardonnay wine
¼	cup flour
2	quarts chicken stock
	Sea salt or kosher salt
	Freshly ground black pepper
¼	cup half and half
2	tablespoons brandy, sherry or Madeira
	Croutons for garnish
	Chopped scallions for garnish

In a large saucepan, melt 2 tablespoons of the butter and sauté onion and garlic for 1 minute. Add carrots, mushrooms, dill and tarragon, cover and simmer over low heat until vegetables are tender. Remove from heat.

In a separate pan, poach the shrimp in the Chardonnay for 3 to 5 minutes, just until they are pink. Chop them finely and add to the vegetables.

In a third pan, melt the remaining butter and stir in flour; cook, stirring continuously, until the mixture is a pale tan color. Cool slightly, slowly add chicken stock while continuing to stir, and bring to a boil. Reduce heat, simmer for 2 minutes, then add to the shrimp and vegetable mixture. Stir. Simmer 20 minutes more.

Pour soup in a food processor or blender and process until smooth. Just before serving, bring soup to a boil, add half and half and brandy, sherry or Madeira and simmer 2 minutes.

NOTE: Do not allow soup to boil once cream has been added or it will curdle.

Garnish with croutons and chopped scallions.

Serves 10

Serve with Chardonnay.

Poached Egg Soup

4	**slices white toast, buttered**
4	**eggs**
2	**tablespoons grated Parmesan cheese**
4	**cups hot beef or chicken broth**
2	**tablespoons Chardonnay wine**

Preheat oven to 375° F.

Place slices of toast in four individual casseroles. Break egg on top of each slice and sprinkle with ½ tablespoon cheese. Combine broth and wine and pour over eggs. Place in oven for about 7 minutes or until eggs are lightly poached.

Serves 4

Serve with Chardonnay.

Vegetable Bean Soup with Pistou

Pistou is the French version of pesto.

1   tablespoon butter
1   tablespoon olive oil
1   medium onion, chopped
2   large leeks, chopped
2   cloves garlic, minced
2   large carrots, sliced
2   large potatoes, peeled and diced
10 cups chicken stock
1   teaspoon sea salt or kosher salt
    Pistou (recipe follows)
1   cup Chardonnay wine
¼   pound Swiss chard, chopped
½   pound green beans, cut into 1-inch pieces
2   medium tomatoes, coarsely chopped
2   zucchini, halved lengthwise and thinly sliced
2   cups cooked, small, dried white beans
1   cup soup macaroni, small size

In a large stock pot, heat the butter and oil; add the onion, leeks, garlic and carrots. Sauté the vegetables for 5 minutes; add the potatoes, chicken stock and salt. Bring the soup to a boil, reduce heat and simmer, uncovered, for 30 minutes. Meanwhile, prepare Pistou.

PISTOU

3 cloves garlic	¼ cup olive oil
1 cup fresh basil leaves	⅓ cup grated Parmesan cheese

In a food processor, purée garlic and basil, then gradually add olive oil. Transfer mixture to a bowl, and stir in cheese. Set Pistou aside.

To the soup pot, add wine, Swiss chard, green beans, tomatoes, zucchini, cooked beans and pasta. Bring to a boil. Reduce the heat and simmer until the pasta is cooked, about 8 to 10 minutes. Stir in half the Pistou, saving the rest to serve at the table. Season the soup with pepper and additional salt, if desired.

Serves 10 to 12

Enjoy with a Chardonnay.

Bow Ties in Broth

¾   **cup small bow-tie pasta (tripolini) or other small pasta**
4   **cups chicken broth**
½   **cup Chardonnay wine**
2   **tablespoons Parmesan cheese**
1   **scallion, including top, finely chopped**

Cook pasta in 1 quart of water for 10 to 12 minutes.

Meanwhile, combine broth and Chardonnay; heat to boiling. Reduce heat and simmer for 5 minutes. When pasta is cooked, drain and add to broth.

To serve, ladle soup into individual bowls and sprinkle with Parmesan cheese and scallion.

Serves 4

Serve with Chardonnay.

Rice and Potato Soup

3	tablespoons olive oil
½	medium onion, finely chopped
2	tablespoons fresh chopped parsley
1½	pounds (about 6 medium-sized) Idaho potatoes, peeled and thinly sliced
2	quarts beef or chicken broth
½	cup Chardonnay wine
1	cup rice
1	teaspoon sea salt or kosher salt
½	teaspoon black pepper
½	cup lean cooked ham, finely chopped

In a large saucepan, heat olive oil to medium-hot and sauté onion and parsley just until onion is soft. Add potatoes and 1 cup broth, cover and simmer for 15 minutes. Add remaining broth, Chardonnay, salt and pepper. Add rice when broth starts to boil. Reduce heat and simmer for 15 to 18 minutes, stirring occasionally. Add ham and simmer 5 minutes more.

Serves 6 to 8

Serve with Chardonnay.

14

Pastas &
Grains

Fettuccine with Lemon Caper Sauce

1	6-ounce package fettuccine pasta
2	strips fresh lemon peel
8	tablespoons butter
2	cloves garlic, crushed
½	cup Chardonnay wine
1	tablespoon lemon juice
2	tablespoons capers
2	tablespoons minced fresh basil
½	teaspoon cornstarch
¼	cup water
¼	cup grated Parmesan cheese
2	tablespoons minced fresh parsley

In a 2-quart saucepan, bring water to boil and add lemon peel strips. Add pasta and cook al dente according to package directions. Drain and discard lemon peel.

In a large skillet over medium heat, melt butter and sauté garlic until slightly browned. Remove garlic and discard. Stir in Chardonnay wine, lemon juice, capers and basil. Heat just until hot. Combine cornstarch and water, blending to a smooth paste, then gradually pour into the hot wine sauce and simmer for a few minute until slightly thickened. Toss with hot pasta. Add Parmesan cheese and toss well. Sprinkle with parsley before serving.

Serves 4

Serve with Chardonnay.

Fettuccine with Crab and Vegetables

½   pound crabmeat
    Juice of 1 lemon
1   tablespoon olive oil
1   pound sweet unsalted butter
3   cloves garlic, minced
1   medium leek, finely chopped (include pale green part)
2   tablespoons minced shallot
3   green onions, finely chopped
1   teaspoon dried tarragon
1   bay leaf
    Sea salt or kosher salt and pepper to taste
1   cup Chardonnay wine
3   medium tomatoes, peeled, seeded, and diced
    Pinch of baking soda
¼   cup sherry
1   cup whipping cream
1   tablespoon minced parsley for garnish
10 ounces fettuccine

In a small bowl, break the crabmeat into bite-sized pieces and sprinkle with lemon juice. Heat olive oil in a non-reactive saucepan over medium heat. Add butter and heat until bubbling but not brown. Add garlic, leek, shallot and green onions. Crumble tarragon and add to saucepan along with bay leaf and salt and pepper to taste. Cook, stirring occasionally, until vegetables are crisp-tender.

Add Chardonnay wine and increase heat. Reduce the sauce by about half. Add diced tomato and salt lightly. Add a pinch of baking soda. Heat, stirring, for 1-2 minutes. Add sherry and bring to a boil. Add cream and continue to boil for a few minutes more, until sauce has reached desired consistency. Add crabmeat and chives, blend, and heat to a simmer. Remove bay leaf.

Cook pasta according to package directions; drain. Place on individual plates, top with sauce, and sprinkle with parsley.

Serves 4

Serve with Chardonnay.

Linguine with Shrimp Sauté

2	tablespoons olive oil
2	cloves garlic, minced
1	pound large shrimp, shelled and deveined
¼	cup Chardonnay wine
¼	cup finely chopped sun-dried tomatoes
½	cup sliced mushrooms
1	teaspoon sea salt or kosher salt
¼	teaspoon ground white pepper
2	tablespoons minced parsley
10	ounces linguine, cooked

In a large skillet, heat olive oil; sauté garlic for 1 minute. Add the shrimp and sauté just until pink. Add the Chardonnay, sun-dried tomatoes and mushrooms; cook until mixture begins to simmer. Stir in salt and pepper. Mix gently with cooked linguine, sprinkle with parsley, and serve.

Serves 4

Serve with Chardonnay.

Pasta Bolognese

Most of the ingredients in this excellent recipe can be easily prepared in a food processor.

6	slices bacon, diced
1	medium onion, finely chopped
2	cloves garlic, minced
1	stalk celery, finely chopped
½	cup chopped fresh parsley
½	cup chopped fresh basil or ½ teaspoon dried basil
1	carrot, diced
½	teaspoon rosemary
½	teaspoon oregano
2	tablespoons butter
¼	pound chicken livers, cut into small pieces
1	pound ground round steak
1	teaspoon sea salt or kosher salt
1	teaspoon black pepper
¼	teaspoon nutmeg
5	ripe Roma tomatoes, chopped, or ½ cup tomato sauce
1½	cups beef bouillon
1	cup sliced mushrooms
½	cup Chardonnay wine
	Spaghetti, cooked, to serve 6
	Parmesan cheese

Sauté mushrooms in butter. Set aside.

In a large heavy pan, fry bacon and drain off most of fat. Add onion, garlic, celery, parsley, basil, carrot and dried herbs. Cook over low heat until soft. Push to side of pan, add butter and chicken livers. Brown lightly. Add ground round steak, cook and stir until well browned, 10 to 15 minutes. Season with salt, black pepper and nutmeg. Stir in tomatoes, or tomato sauce, and bouillon. Cover and simmer gently for 30 minutes. Add mushrooms and Chardonnay; simmer 30 minutes more.

Serve over spaghetti. Top with Parmesan cheese.

Serves 6

Serve with Chardonnay.

Rice with Sage and Chardonnay

1	16-ounce package long-grain rice
¼	pound butter
1	clove garlic, crushed
½	teaspoon powdered sage
½	cup dry Chardonnay wine
½	cup grated Parmesan cheese

Cook rice according to package directions.

About 5 minutes before rice is done, in a large saucepan over medium heat, melt butter. (Keep heat low enough so butter does not turn brown.) Gently sauté garlic and sage in butter, until garlic is lightly golden. Remove and discard garlic. Add Chardonnay and simmer, stirring occasionally, until sauce is reduced by half.

Place hot rice in a large serving dish, pour sauce over it, and mix well. Sprinkle with cheese and serve.

Serves 4 to 6

Serve with Chardonnay.

Tortellini with Chardonnay Herb Sauce

2   9-ounce packages uncooked fresh refrigerated
      cheese-filled spinach tortellini
¼   cup butter
1   small onion, finely chopped
2   cloves garlic, minced
1   small red bell pepper, chopped
2   tablespoons flour
1½   cups half and half
¼   cup dry Chardonnay wine
1   teaspoon dry Italian herb seasoning
¼   teaspoon sea salt or kosher salt
¼   teaspoon white pepper
½   cup grated Parmesan cheese

Cook tortellini according to package directions. Drain. Keep warm.

In a 2-quart saucepan, melt butter and sauté onion, garlic and red bell pepper until soft. Stir in flour until smooth and bubbly, about 30 seconds. Add half and half, Chardonnay, Italian seasoning, salt and pepper. Continue cooking, stirring occasionally, until sauce thickens, 5 to 8 minutes. Adjust seasoning and stir in additional Chardonnay if desired.

Serve sauce over hot cooked tortellini; top with Parmesan cheese.

Serves 6

Serve with Chardonnay.

Linguine with Mushrooms

3	tablespoons butter
2½	cups sliced fresh mushrooms
1	clove garlic, minced
½	cup sliced green onion
½	cup dry Chardonnay
¼	teaspoon dried basil
½	teaspoon sea salt or kosher salt
¼	teaspoon white pepper
¹/₃	cup heavy cream or half and half
1	8-ounce package linquine
	Chopped fresh parsley for garnish

In a 2-quart saucepan over medium heat, melt butter and sauté mushrooms, garlic and onion until tender. Stir in Chardonnay, basil, salt and pepper. Bring to a boil. Reduce heat and simmer, uncovered, for 25 to 30 minutes or until liquid evaporates. Stir in cream; heat just until mixture thickens slightly.

Meanwhile, cook linguine al dente according to package directions. Drain and transfer to a serving bowl. Pour mushroom mixture over linguine; toss to coat. Sprinkle with parsley.

Makes 8 side-dish servings

Serve with Chardonnay.

Pasta with Prosciutto and Asparagus

½   pound fresh young asparagus, trimmed
4   ounces prosciutto or other cured ham, thinly sliced
    and cut into 1-inch strips
¼   cup freshly grated Parmesan cheese
¼   cup freshly grated Romano cheese
½   cup sour cream
¼   cup Chardonnay wine
¼   cup (½ cube) butter, melted
½   pound linguine or fettuccine

In a medium saucepan, steam asparagus until crisp-tender. Drain and cut into bite-sized pieces. Set aside.

In a medium bowl, combine asparagus and prosciutto.

In a large bowl, combine cheeses, sour cream, Chardonnay and melted butter. Mix well. Add asparagus-prosciutto mixture; stir.

Cook pasta according to package directions. Drain well. Transfer pasta to a warm serving platter and toss with sauce.

Serves 4

Serve with Chardonnay.

Penne Pasta with Fresh Green Beans

4   slices bacon
12   ounces penne pasta
1   pound tender fresh green beans, strings removed, cut or snapped into bite-sized pieces
1   small onion, finely chopped
2   cloves garlic, minced
2   tablespoons flour
½   cup Chardonnay wine
½   cup chicken broth
2   tablespoons lemon juice
2   large tomatoes, chopped
½   cup snipped fresh basil
½   cup finely shredded Parmesan cheese

In a large skillet, cook bacon until crisp. Remove bacon from pan, drain on paper towels, crumble, and set aside. Reserve 2 tablespoons bacon drippings in skillet.

Cook pasta according to package directions, adding green beans during the last 5 minutes of cooking. Drain and transfer pasta-green bean mixture to a large serving dish; keep warm.

While pasta is cooking, add onion and garlic to reserved bacon drippings in skillet and cook until tender. Stir in flour to make a smooth paste. Stir in Chardonnay, broth, and lemon juice; bring to a boil. Reduce heat and simmer, uncovered, for 5 minutes or until sauce is reduced by half. Add wine mixture, tomatoes, and basil to pasta; toss. Sprinkle with Parmesan cheese and crumbled bacon. Serve.

Serves 4

Serve with Chardonnay.

Baked Rice with Cheese and Mushrooms

4	cups cooked rice
4	tablespoons butter
4	tablespoons flour
2	cups half-and-half
1	cup grated cheddar cheese (medium-sharp)
1	cup sliced pimiento-stuffed olives
1	cup sliced fresh mushrooms
½	small green bell pepper, finely chopped
½	small red bell pepper, finely chopped
4	hard-cooked eggs, sliced
½	cup Chardonnay wine
1	teaspoon sea salt or kosher salt
½	teaspoon black pepper

Preheat oven to 375° F.

Cook rice and keep it warm.

While rice is cooking, cook sauce. In a large saucepan over medium heat, melt butter. Stir in flour and cook until mixture begins to boil. Gradually add half and half, stirring continuously, until mixture returns to boiling point. Reduce heat and simmer, continuing to stir, until sauce thickens slightly. Add ½ cup of the grated cheese and stir until melted.

Combine cooked rice and sauce. Stir in remaining ingredients in order given. Pour into individual greased casseroles or one large greased casserole. Sprinkle remaining cheese on top.

Bake for 25 to 30 minutes.

Serves 6

Serve with Chardonnay.

Smoked Salmon Pasta Salad

1	package (16 ounces) shell macaroni
¼	cup fresh lemon juice
¼	cup Chardonnay wine
1	tablespoon lemon zest
2	teaspoons dry dillweed
4	teaspoons Dijon-style mustard
2	teaspoons granulated sugar
½	teaspoon kosher salt
¼	teaspoon white pepper
3	tablespoons peanut oil
6	ounces flaked hot smoked salmon, skinned and boned
½	cup coarsely chopped cucumber
3	green onions, finely chopped
2	tablespoons capers

In a medium saucepan, cook pasta according to package directions; drain. Rinse in cold water and drain again. Transfer pasta to a large serving dish; set aside.

In a small bowl, whisk together the lemon juice, lemon zest, Chardonnay, dillweed, mustard, sugar, salt and pepper. Slowly add peanut oil in a thin, steady stream, whisking continuously.

Add the salmon, cucumber, green onion and capers to the pasta. Pour on dressing and toss gently to blend ingredients and flavors. Sprinkle with additional dillweed. Serve immediately ... on a bed of lettuce if desired.

Serves 6

Serve with Chardonnay.

27

Curried Chicken Pasta Salad

1   16-ounce package rotini pasta
1   red apple, finely chopped
1   can (1 lb. 4 oz.) pineapple tidbits, drained and chilled
1   cup white seedless grapes, halved and chilled
½   cup raisins
2   tablespoons lemon juice
6   cups shredded lettuce

DRESSING
¾   cup mayonnaise
1   tablespoon honey
1   tablespoon Chardonnay wine
2   teaspoons curry powder
1   teaspoon sesame oil
2   cups cubed cooked chicken breast meat (To avoid
     cooking and save time, use a lemon- or garlic-flavored
     rotisserie chicken from the grocery store deli.)
2   tablespoons cashew pieces

In a medium saucepan, cook pasta according to package directions; drain. Rinse in cold water and drain again. Transfer pasta to a large serving dish; set aside.

Combine apple, pineapple, grapes, raisins, and lemon juice. Arrange shredded lettuce on a large platter. Place fruit on top.

For dressing, combine mayonnaise, honey, Chardonnay, curry powder, and sesame oil. Add chicken and pasta and stir gently to combine. Spoon atop fruit on platter. Sprinkle with cashews.

Serves 4 to 6

Serve with Chardonnay.

28

Papa's Quick Vegetable Garden Polenta

2   tablespoons butter
1   16-ounce package purchased polenta, any flavor, cut into 12 slices
½   cup Chardonnay wine
2   cups (about 1 pound) fresh green beans, cut or snapped into bite-sized pieces
1   cup sliced fresh mushrooms
1   cup sliced fresh zucchini
½   teaspoon sea salt or kosher salt
1   large fresh ripe tomato, chopped
½   cup fresh shredded basil leaves, firmly packed
¼   cup grated Parmesan cheese
¼   cup shredded Mozzarella cheese

In a heavy skillet over medium heat, melt 1 tablespoon of butter. Sauté polenta slices, turning once, until golden brown, 8 to 10 minutes. Remove polenta to a serving dish and keep warm.

In the same skillet, heat 1 tablespoon butter until bubbly. Add Chardonnay wine, green beans, mushrooms, zucchini and salt. Sauté over medium heat until vegetables are crisp-tender, about 6 minutes. Spoon vegetables over and around the sliced polenta, allowing portions of the polenta to remain visible.

Combine fresh chopped tomato and shredded basil leaves; spoon over and around cooked vegetables. Sprinkle Parmesan and Mozzarella cheeses over all.

Serves 4 to 6

Serve with Chardonnay.

Chardonnay Rice Salad with Chicken

3	cups cooked long grain rice
1	small can sliced black olives, drained
¼	cup finely chopped green bell pepper
¼	cup finely chopped red bell pepper
½	cup canned garbanzo beans, drained
1	scallion, thinly sliced
1	small jar (6.5 ounces) marinated artichoke hearts
2	chicken breasts, skinned and boned
2	teaspoons chili powder
½	teaspoon dried rosemary
½	teaspoon dried thyme
½	teaspoon lemon salt
2	teaspoons lemon juice
¼	cup Chardonnay wine
½	cup crumbled feta cheese

In a large bowl, combine olives, green and red bell peppers, garbanzo beans, and scallion. Drain artichokes, reserving marinade, then chop artichokes. Combine vegetables with rice.

Cut chicken into bite-sized chunks. Sprinkle with chili powder, rosemary, thyme, and lemon salt. In a large skillet over medium heat, bring reserved artichoke marinade, lemon juice and Chardonnay to a boil. Reduce heat and simmer chicken for 3 to 4 minutes or until well cooked. Add chicken to rice mixture; add additional marinade to moisten to taste; add feta cheese; toss gently. Chill for several hours or overnight before serving.

Serves 4 to 6

Serve with Chardonnay.

Meats

Curried Lamb Stew

½   cup cooking oil
2   pounds lamb stew meat
$^1/_3$ cup flour
1   tablespoon curry powder
½   teaspoon cumin
1   cup water
1   cup Chardonnay
2   teaspoons sea salt or kosher salt
¼   teaspoon black pepper
$^1/_8$ teaspoon garlic salt
1   large yellow onion, thinly sliced
3   cups peeled baby carrots

In a large, heavy pan, heat oil to medium hot. Add meat and brown well. Remove meat from pan. Blend flour, curry and cumin into drippings. Add water and wine; cook, stirring continuously, until mixture is thick and smooth. Add salt, pepper and garlic salt.

Return meat to pan and top with onion slices. Cover and simmer 1½ hours, or until meat is tender. Add baby carrots to pan during last 10 to 15 minutes; cook until crisp-tender.

It's a good idea to make this dish early in the day and chill so you can remove the top fat. Reheat stew before serving. Serve with rice and a green salad.

Serves 4 to 6

Serve with Chardonnay.

Veal Goulash

1½ pounds veal cutlet or veal stew meat
3   tablespoons olive oil
1   large onion, chopped
1   clove garlic, minced
1   tablespoon butter
8   ounces fresh small mushrooms
¾   cup red bell pepper, chopped
1½ cups chicken broth
½   cup Chardonnay wine
1   teaspoon sea salt or kosher salt
¼   teaspoon black pepper
1   tablespoon paprika
1   cup sour cream

Cube veal into bite-size pieces. Heat olive oil in a large saucepan over medium-high heat; sauté veal, onion and garlic until golden. Set aside.

In a smaller pan, melt butter and sauté mushrooms and red bell pepper. Set aside.

Add chicken broth, Chardonnay, salt, pepper and paprika to veal. Cover and simmer gently for 1 hour. Adjust seasoning to taste. Drain mushrooms and add to veal. Remove pan from heat. Before serving, stir in sour cream. Do not let it boil.

Delicious with buttered noodles.

Serves 4

Serve with Chardonnay.

Quick Pepper Steak

2	tablespoons olive oil
1	pound round steak (beef, deer, or elk), cut into cubes or strips
1	large onion, diced
1	clove garlic, minced
1	green pepper, chopped
1½	cups chopped celery
2	tablespoons cornstarch
6	tablespoons soy sauce
1	teaspoon sea salt or kosher salt
½	teaspoon black pepper
4	beef bouillon cubes
1	cup Chardonnay wine
3	cups water
1	cup sliced mushrooms
1	cup peeled baby carrots
3	medium tomatoes, peeled, seeded, chopped

In a large skillet, heat olive oil to medium-hot and sauté meat until browned. Remove meat from pan and add onion, garlic, green pepper and celery. Cook and stir over high heat for 2 minutes. Mix cornstarch with soy sauce and add to pan. Add remaining ingredients. Return meat to pan. Cover, reduce heat, and simmer 30 minutes. If sauce needs additional thickening, mix 1 to 2 tablespoons more cornstarch with a small amount of water, then blend into the gravy.

Serve over rice or cooked noodles.   Serves 4 to 6

Serve with Chardonnay.

Veal Valentino

8	(about 1½ pounds) veal cutlets, thinly cut and boneless
2	tablespoons olive oil
1	tablespoon flour
1	cup chicken stock
1	cup light cream
	Sea salt or kosher salt
	Black pepper
¼	pound (about 1 cup) mushrooms, sliced
2	tablespoons lemon juice
¼	cup Chardonnay wine
1	pound fresh asparagus, cooked
4	small zucchini, peeled and cut in 2-inch strips
2	tablespoons butter
2	tablespoons grated Parmesan cheese

In a large skillet, heat olive oil to medium-hot. Sauté veal cutlets for 3 to 4 minutes on each side or until they are brown. Remove from skillet and keep warm.

Stir flour into the skillet liquid; cook, stirring constantly, until flour is lightly browned. Stir in chicken stock and cream, season with salt and pepper, and bring to a boil. Add the sliced mushrooms, lemon juice and Chardonnay, and return veal cutlets to the skillet. Simmer over low heat for 5 to 6 minutes until veal is tender. Add the cooked asparagus and cook 1 to 2 minutes longer until very hot.

Blanche the zucchini in boiling salted water for 1 minute, drain and cook quickly in melted butter in a covered pan for 1 to 2 minutes, until tender-crisp. Season with salt and pepper.

Spoon the zucchini into an ovenproof casserole, lay the veal on top. Adjust sauce seasonings in skillet and pour over meat. Arrange the asparagus on top, sprinkle with Parmesan cheese and broil until browned.

Serve with boiled small new potatoes tossed in butter and parsley.

Serves 4

Serve with Chardonnay.

Chardonnay Ham Glaze

½	cup Chardonnay wine	10	dried apricots, chopped
¾	cup grape juice	1	tablespoon cornstarch
¼	cup orange juice	½	teaspoon dry mustard
½	cup raisins	2	tablespoons cold water
	Zest of 1 lemon	¼	teaspoon mace
	Zest of 1 orange	¼	teaspoon nutmeg
¼	cup slivered almonds		

In a small saucepan, simmer Chardonnay, grape and orange juice, raisins and fruit zest for 10 minutes until raisins are plumped and liquid starts to reduce. Add almonds and apricots.

In a separate small bowl, mix cornstarch, mustard and 2 tablespoons cold water. Add 3 tablespoons of the hot fruit-glaze mixture to the cornstarch mixture. Stir well and pour into fruit-glaze mixture in pan. Cook, stirring for 1 minute. Add mace and nutmeg. Serve with finished ham.

Makes 1 cup

Serve with Chardonnay.

Roast Pork Dijonnaise

3   pounds fresh pork loin, fat trimmed to ½-inch layer
1   tablespoon Dijon-style mustard
1½ teaspoons brown sugar
2   tablespoons Chardonnay wine
¼   cup dry white bread crumbs
12 whole cloves

SAUCE
1   small onion, finely chopped
2½ tablespoons butter
1   tablespoon flour
1½ cups chicken stock
½   cup Chardonnay wine
2   teaspoons tomato paste
2   cups (½ pound) mushrooms, sliced
     Sea salt or kosher salt

Preheat oven to 375° F. Blend mustard, sugar and Chardonnay to a paste, spread over fat top of pork, press on bread crumbs and stud meat with cloves. Put meat on a rack in roasting pan and roast for 1¾ hours, or until meat thermometer registers 185° F. Baste meat every 20 minutes or so while cooking.

For sauce, melt 1½ tablespoons butter in a large skillet; sauté onion until translucent. Stir in flour and cook until mixture is brown. Add chicken stock, wine, and tomato paste and bring to a boil. Reduce heat and simmer for 12 to 15 minutes to thicken sauce. In another small pan, sauté mushrooms in remaining butter for 1 minute; add to the sauce and adjust seasoning to taste. Serve sauce with meat.

Serve with Chardonnay.   Serves 4 to 6

Broiled Mushroom-Stuffed Lamb Chops

10 lamb chops, thickly cut
    Butter to brush on chops

STUFFING
2   tablespoons butter
½   yellow onion, finely chopped
3   cups (¾ pound) mushrooms, finely chopped
¼   cup Chardonnay wine
1   clove garlic, minced
1   tablespoon chopped fresh parsley
½   teaspoon dried thyme
     Sea salt or kosher salt
     Ground black pepper

Trussing needle and string ... or use toothpicks

Stuffing: In a heavy skillet over medium-high heat, melt butter. Add onion and cook until translucent. Add mushrooms and Chardonnay; cook, uncovered, stirring frequently, until all liquid has evaporated. Stir in the garlic, cook 30 seconds longer, remove from heat, add herbs, and salt and pepper. Let cool.

With a small, sharp pointed knife, cut a large pocket in each chop; fill with cooled stuffing and fasten with trussing. **NOTE:** Do not stuff chops more than 2 hours before cooking.

Brush chops with butter and broil 4 to 5 inches from burner for 7 to 8 minutes per side, turning once. Brush often with butter.

Serve with Chardonnay.   Serves 10

Spicy Spareribs

4	pounds spareribs, cracked through center
1/3	cup flour
2	teaspoons sea salt or kosher salt
1/2	teaspoon black pepper
3	tablespoons cooking oil
1½	cups meat broth, or hot water with 1 bouillon cube
1	cup Chardonnay wine
1/4	cup ketchup
3½	tablespoons Worcestershire sauce
2	tablespoons cider vinegar
2	tablespoons maple syrup
1/2	teaspoon celery salt
1/4	teaspoon cayenne pepper
2	cloves garlic, minced
1	medium onion, chopped

Preheat oven to 350° F. Cut spareribs into serving-sized pieces. Coat evenly with a mixture of flour, salt and pepper. Heat oil in a heavy skillet over medium heat; brown meat and place in a roasting pan with a tight-fitting lid.

In a bowl, mix together meat broth, Chardonnay, ketchup, Worcestershire sauce, vinegar, syrup, celery salt, cayenne, and garlic. Pour over browned ribs. Add chopped onion. Roast, covered, for 1½ hours. Remove meat from pan.

For gravy, remove excess fat from pan, pour juices into a small pan and thicken with cornstarch according to package directions.

Serves 4 to 6

Serve with Chardonnay.

Roast Pork Tenderloin Chardonnay

2   pounds pork tenderloin
1   tablespoon Dijon mustard
1   teaspoon brown sugar
1   teaspoon dried thyme
1   teaspoon sea salt or kosher salt
½   teaspoon black pepper
2   tablespoons olive oil
1   cup dry Chardonnay wine
1   cup heavy cream or half and half
2   tablespoons fresh chopped parsley

Preheat oven to 350° F.

Pat pork tenderloin dry. Combine mustard, brown sugar, thyme, salt and pepper. Rub into pork.

In a roasting pan that can be used on direct heat and in the oven, heat oil to medium-high and brown meat on all sides. Add Chardonnay to the pan and roast in oven for 45 to 50 minutes or until meat thermometer registers 160° F.

Remove meat from pan; keep warm. Add cream to pan juices and scrape up bits of meat stuck to the bottom of the pan, stirring them into the sauce. Bring sauce to a boil and simmer gently until slightly thickened. Adjust seasonings to taste.

Slice pork and return it to the sauce. Heat gently before serving. Garnish with chopped parsley.

Serves 6

Serve with dry Chardonnay.

Quick Veal with Herbs and Chardonnay

2	pounds lean veal
2	teaspoons flour
1	tablespoon butter
1	clove garlic, minced
1¼	teaspoons Italian seasoning
½	teaspoon dried marjoram
¼	teaspoon nutmeg
1	teaspoon salt
3	tablespoons cornstarch
½	cup water
½	cup heavy cream
½	cup dry Chardonnay wine

Cut veal into bite-sized pieces and dredge with flour. In a large frying pan over high heat, melt the butter and sauté veal and garlic until golden brown. Sprinkle meat mixture with seasonings while it is cooking. Reduce heat to low and allow to simmer.

Stir cornstarch into 1 tablespoon of the water. Add the remaining water to the cornstarch mixture. Pour slowly into meat mixture, stirring continuously. Stir in cream and Chardonnay. Cover and cook 10 minutes or until mixture thickens slightly. Do not boil.

Serve over rice or noodles.

Serves 4

Serve with Chardonnay.

Beef Stew Romana

2	pounds lean beef stew meat
1½	tablespoons cooking oil
4	slices bacon, finely chopped
1	clove garlic, minced
1	medium onion, chopped
¼	teaspoon dried marjoram
½	teaspoon dried oregano
½	cup Chardonnay wine
2	tablespoons tomato paste
1	teaspoon sea salt or kosher salt
½	teaspoon black pepper

In a large stock pot, heat cooking oil to medium high and sauté bacon, garlic, and onion until garlic and onion are tender. Add meat, sprinkle with salt, pepper, marjoram and oregano; brown on all sides.

Add Chardonnay to stock pot and cook stew over medium heat until wine has evaporated. Pour in tomato paste and simmer, uncovered, for 10 minutes. Add enough warm water to cover meat.

Cover saucepan tightly and simmer for 2 hours or until meat is tender. Add more water during cooking if necessary.

Serves 4 to 6

Serve with Chardonnay.

Veal Stew with Tomatoes and Chardonnay

2   pounds lamb stew meat or veal rump meat cut into
       1½-inch cubes
⅓   cup olive oil
1   clove garlic, minced
1   teaspoon sea salt or kosher salt
¼   teaspoon black pepper
1   bay leaf, crumbled
1   tablespoon fresh basil, finely chopped, or ¼ teaspoon
       dried basil
1   cup dry Chardonnay
6   Roma tomatoes, diced, or 2 tablespoons tomato paste
½   cup peeled baby carrots

In a heavy skillet, heat olive oil to medium-hot and sauté garlic until soft. Add meat and brown on all sides. Add salt, pepper, bay leaf, and basil. Cook 1 to 2 minutes. Add Chardonnay.

Cook over medium-high heat until wine has evaporated. Add tomatoes or tomato paste. Cover and simmer for about 1½ hours until meat is tender, adding a little water during cooking if necessary. Add baby carrots during last ½ hour of cooking.

Serves 4

Serve with Chardonnay.

Poultry

Chicken with Mushrooms and Artichoke Hearts

2   **tablespoons butter**
4   **boneless, skinless chicken breasts, lightly floured**
½   **cup sliced fresh mushrooms**
8   **artichoke hearts from a can, quartered**
2   **teaspoons chopped fresh basil**
2   **tablespoons lemon juice**
½   **cup Chardonnay wine**
      Fresh chopped parsley for garnish
      Basil sprigs for garnish

In a medium skillet or sauté pan over medium heat, melt butter. Add the chicken, mushrooms and artichoke hearts. Sauté 3 to 4 minutes; turn chicken over. Add basil and cook, uncovered, until chicken is done. Add lemon juice and Chardonnay wine and simmer, uncovered, until liquid is reduced and thickened.

Place the chicken breasts on a warm platter and cover with mushroom-and-artichoke sauce. Garnish with chopped parsley and a sprig of basil.

Serves 4

Serve with Chardonnay.

Chicken Chardonnay

4	ounces sweet butter
1	clove garlic, minced
¼	cup shallots, minced
2	teaspoons dill weed
¾	cup Chardonnay wine
4	chicken breasts (2 whole) skinned, boned and lightly pounded flat
½	teaspoon sea salt or kosher salt
¼	teaspoon white pepper
3	cups fresh peeled baby carrots
2	zucchini, cut on the diagonal in thin rounds
1	cup sour cream
1	teaspoon cornstarch
12	cherry tomatoes
2	tablespoons chopped parsley

In a large skillet with a lid, melt butter and add garlic, shallots and dill weed. Sauté 2 minutes over medium heat. Add Chardonnay and bring to a boil. Season chicken with salt and pepper and add to pan. Poach, covered, 3 to 4 minutes per side. Remove chicken to heated platter and keep warm. Simmer pan liquid until reduced by one-third.

Add baby carrots to pan; poach, covered, about 6 minutes. Add zucchini to pan; poach, covered, about 5 minutes more, until both carrots and zucchini are crisp-tender. Arrange vegetables around chicken on a heated platter.

Place sour cream in a small bowl and whisk in cornstarch. Slowly whisk hot pan juices into the sour cream until well blended. Return sauce to pan and whisk about 2 minutes over low heat, or until it thickens. Adjust seasonings. Add tomatoes and heat until they are just warmed through. Pour sauce over chicken and vegetables. Sprinkle with chopped parsley.

Serves 4

Serve with Chardonnay.

Stuffed Quail

1	small package wild and long grain rice, cooked
8	quail
16	strips uncooked bacon
2	tablespoons butter
½	cup Chardonnay wine
1	cube beef bouillon
	Salt and pepper
	Green grapes for garnish

Preheat oven to 350° F. Wash quail and pat dry. Stuff with cooked rice. Wrap 2 strips of bacon around each quail. In a large skillet, melt butter and fry quail until slightly brown. Place in pan and bake for 25 minutes.

While quail bake, remove all but ½ cup oil from pan. Add Chardonnay and cook over medium heat for 2 to 3 minutes. Add bouillon cube. Simmer 5 minutes. Salt and pepper to taste. When quail are done, place on a platter and cover with sauce. Garnish with grapes.

Serves 4

Serve with Chardonnay.

49

Game Hens with Croissant Stuffing

6   Cornish game hens
1   large egg, beaten
12 day-old croissants, pulled apart
1   cup yellow raisins
¾   cup water chestnuts, chopped
1   medium yellow onion, diced
5   stalks celery, diced
2   medium apples, cored and diced
1   tablespoon poultry seasoning
½   tablespoon cinnamon
2   cups chicken stock
1   teaspoon each kosher salt and black pepper
1   cube butter
1   cup water
1   bottle Chardonnay wine
     Orange slices and fresh mint leaves for garnish

Wash and pat dry game hens; set aside. Combine egg, croissants, raisins, water chestnuts, onion, celery, apple, poultry seasoning, salt, pepper, and cinnamon in a bowl. Add stock a little at a time until mixture takes on a sticky consistency.

Rub hens with butter and stuff with above mixture. Place them in a long, foil-lined baking pan. Pour Chardonnay over hens. Add water to bottom of pan as needed. Salt and pepper hens to taste. Bake, uncovered, at 350° F for 1 hour, basting every 15 minutes. Garnish with orange slices and fresh mint leaves.

Serves 6

Serve with late harvest Chardonnay.

Chicken Breasts with Shrimp Sauce

8	chicken breasts
½	cup milk
4	tablespoons butter

SHRIMP SAUCE

4	tablespoons butter
⅓	cup flour
1	cup milk
½	teaspoon sea salt or kosher salt
¼	teaspoon white pepper
¼	teaspoon seafood seasoning
1½	cups cooked shrimp, cut into small pieces
1	cup fresh mushrooms, thinly sliced
1	teaspoon paprika
½	cup Chardonnay wine
1½	tablespoons Worcestershire sauce

Preheat oven to 350° F. Wash and pat dry chicken and place in roasting pan. Pour milk over chicken and place ½ tablespoon butter on each piece. Cover tightly with foil and bake 1 hour.

For shrimp sauce, melt 4 tablespoons butter over low heat. Stir in flour until well blended, then add 1 cup milk slowly and stir until thickened. Add salt, pepper, and seafood seasoning. Add shrimp, mushrooms, paprika, Chardonnay and Worcestershire sauce. Stir over low heat for 10 minutes. To serve, place a chicken breast on each plate and spoon sauce over top. Sprinkle with paprika.

Serves 6 to 8

Serve with Chardonnay.

51

Mozzarella Chicken Breasts

MARINADE:
1½ cups olive oil
2   cloves garlic, mashed
½   cup Chardonnay wine
1   teaspoon Italian seasoning
½   teaspoon oregano
2   teaspoons lemon juice

1   6-ounce package long grain and wild rice pilaf mix
¼   cup thinly sliced green onions
½   cup water
1   cup broccoli florets
2   teaspoons olive oil
4   marinated chicken breast halves (about 1 pound)
1   medium tomato, halved and thinly sliced
2   slices (3 ounces) mozzarella cheese, halved

Combine marinade ingredients: Olive oil, garlic, Chardonnay, Italian seasoning, oregano and lemon juice. Marinate chicken breasts 4 to 6 hours or overnight.

Cook rice pilaf according to package directions; add green onions the last 5 minutes of cooking. Meanwhile, in a saucepan bring the ½ cup water to boiling; add broccoli florets. Cook, covered, for 3 minutes or until crisp-tender; drain and set aside.

In a large skillet, heat oil and sauté chicken breasts over medium heat for 8 to 10 minutes or until no longer pink, turning once. Overlap the halved tomato slices on top of the chicken breasts.

Spoon cooked broccoli florets on top of tomato slices and cover each with a half-slice of mozzarella cheese.

Broil the chicken breasts 3 to 4 inches from the heat for 1 minute or until cheese is melted and bubbly.

Excellent on hot rice pilaf.

Serves 4

Serve with Chardonnay.

Garlic Chicken

1	**chicken, cut up and skinned**
1	**cup soy sauce**
1	**cup Chardonnay wine**
8	**cloves garlic, crushed**
½	**cup lemon juice**

Preheat oven to 350° F.

Marinate chicken in wine, soy sauce, garlic and lemon juice for 2 hours or overnight. Arrange chicken in a 1½-quart greased baking dish and pour marinade over top. Cover with foil and bake 1 hour, turning pieces once. Serve with rice. Pour marinade over rice for added flavor.

Serves 6

Serve with Chardonnay.

Neptune Chicken Casserole

8   boned chicken breasts, pounded thin
8   ounces sweet unsalted whipped butter
3   large scallions, including tops, finely chopped
6   mushrooms, finely chopped
½   pound white crab meat
¼   pound shrimp
2   teaspoons fresh shredded basil
½   teaspoon grated fresh garlic
¼   teaspoon poultry seasoning
    Sea salt or kosher salt
1   tablespoon lemon juice
½   cup Chardonnay wine
1   teaspoon paprika

SAUCE	4	mushrooms, sliced
	1	scallion, including top, chopped
		Juice of ½ lemon
	½	teaspoon dried dill weed
	3	tablespoons butter

Preheat oven to 350° F. Mix butter, scallions, mushrooms, crabmeat and shrimp. Add spices, lemon juice and salt to taste. Place 2 tablespoons of mixture on each chicken breast and fold corners to cover. Turn over and place in a 3-quart casserole.

Pour Chardonnay over chicken breasts, dot each breast with butter and sprinkle with paprika. Cover the casserole and bake for 15 minutes. Uncover and bake 10 minutes more.

To prepare sauce, pour liquid from casserole into a small pan and bring to a boil. Add mushrooms, scallion, lemon juice and dill and bring to boil again. Lower heat to simmer and reduce liquid by half. Deglaze the sauce by stirring in butter, one tablespoon at a time, with a whisk. Allow sauce to cool slightly. Spoon over each chicken breast.

Delicious over curried rice. Serves 6 to 8

Serve with Chardonnay.

Turkey Piccata

1	pound turkey breast fillets
4	tablespoons butter
2	tablespoons flour
1	cup whipping cream or half and half
½	cup Chardonnay wine
1	tablespoon lemon juice
¼	cup drained capers
	Lemon slices and parsley sprigs for garnish

In a large skillet over medium heat, cook fillets in 2 tablespoons of the butter for 8 to 11 minutes on each side, or until lightly browned and no longer pink in center. Remove from pan and keep warm.

Melt remaining butter in pan; stir in flour and whisk in cream. Simmer until sauce thickens slightly. Slowly stir in wine, lemon juice and capers; heat through. Serve sauce over fillets. Garnish with lemon slices and parsley.

Serves 4

Serve with Chardonnay.

Sonoma Turkey Casserole

6   tablespoons butter
½   cup chopped onion
1   clove garlic, minced
6   mushrooms, sliced
¼   cup chopped green bell pepper
¼   cup chopped red bell pepper
2   tablespoons flour
1½   cups light cream
2   egg yolks
1   teaspoon sea salt or kosher salt
¼   teaspoon freshly ground black pepper
½   cup Chardonnay wine
3   cups cooked, diced turkey
½   pound medium noodles, cooked
½   cup Parmesan cheese

Preheat oven to 350° F.

In heavy skillet over medium heat, melt 4 tablespoons butter. Sauté onion, garlic, mushrooms, and green and red pepper for 5 minutes, stirring frequently. Blend in flour, broth and cream, stirring continuously, until sauce reaches boiling point. Reduce heat and simmer for 5 minutes.

In a bowl, beat egg yolks with salt and pepper and gradually add to hot sauce, stirring steadily to prevent curdling. Mix in Chardonnay, turkey, and noodles. Pour into a 3-quart casserole, sprinkle with cheese and dot with 2 tablespoons butter. Bake for 25 minutes.

Serves 4 to 6

Serve with Chardonnay.

Oriental Chicken

1   chicken breast, cooked
¼   cup orange juice
¼   cup Chardonnay wine
1   tablespoon Chinese style mustard
2   tablespoons soy sauce
½   teaspoon hot sauce
3   tablespoons olive oil
1   medium onion, chopped
1   clove garlic, minced
½   cup mushrooms, chopped
1   can water chestnuts, drained and chopped
½   cup chopped green bell pepper
1   11-ounce can mandarin orange segments, drained

Cut chicken breast into ½-inch cubes and place in bowl.

In separate bowl, combine orange juice, Chardonnay wine, mustard, soy sauce, and hot sauce; pour over chicken and marinate for 2 hours or longer in refrigerator.

In heavy skillet, heat oil; sauté onion, garlic and mushrooms for 1 minute. Remove chicken from marinade with slotted spoon and add to skillet. Cook for 2 minutes, stirring and turning chicken. Add water chestnuts, green bell pepper and remaining marinade. Cook together for 3 minutes. Add orange segments and toss gently until heated through.

Serve with rice.   Serves 4

Serve with Chardonnay.

Deviled Chicken

1   (2 to 3 pounds) frying chicken, cut up (and skinned,
     if desired)
¾   cup flour
1½ teaspoons sea salt or kosher salt
½   teaspoon black pepper
½   teaspoon cayenne pepper
     Cooking oil

SAUCE
2   tablespoons flour
1½ teaspoons dry mustard
     Dash of cayenne pepper
     Dash of bottled hot sauce (optional)
1   cup chicken broth or water
2   teaspoons Worcestershire sauce
1   cup Chardonnay wine

Wash and pat dry chicken. In a plastic bag combine flour, salt, black pepper and cayenne pepper. Place a few chicken pieces at a time in the bag and shake until pieces are evenly coated.

In a large, heavy skillet with a tight-fitting lid, pour cooking oil until it is at least ½-inch deep. Heat oil over medium heat and, starting with meatiest pieces of chicken, fry until brown on all sides. Remove chicken from skillet; set aside and keep warm. Pour off fat and reserve it.

For sauce, return 2 tablespoons chicken drippings to the skillet. Blend in a mixture of 2 tablespoons flour, dry mustard, and dash of cayenne pepper. Heat until mixture bubbles. Remove from heat. Gradually stir in 1 cup chicken broth or water and Worcestershire sauce. Cook rapidly, stirring constantly, until sauce thickens. Blend in Chardonnay wine. Return chicken to skillet, cover, reduce heat and simmer 30 to 40 minutes, or until chicken is tender. Spoon sauce over chicken. Serve with rice or noodles.

Serves 4 to 5

Serve with Chardonnay.

Quick Chick in Chardonnay

1   **frying chicken, cut into serving pieces**
1   **teaspoon sea salt or kosher salt**
½   **teaspoon black pepper**
¼   **cup (½ cube) butter**
1   **cup dry Chardonnay wine**

Wash chicken and pat dry. Sprinkle it with salt and pepper and rub with a couple tablespoons melted butter.

In a large skillet, melt remaining butter. Add chicken to skillet, cover tightly, and cook over medium-high heat for 5 minutes. Turn chicken, cover, and cook 5 minutes more over medium-high heat. Reduce heat and cook for 10 minutes. Add Chardonnay and cook, uncovered, over medium-high heat until wine has evaporated.

Serves 2 to 4

Serve with Chardonnay.

Tango Chicken

1   chicken, whole
1   teaspoon sea salt or kosher salt
½   teaspoon black pepper
1½   teaspoons lime juice
1½   teaspoons lemon juice
3   cloves garlic, minced
2   tablespoons chopped fresh cilantro
½   teaspoon ground cumin
½   teaspoon chili powder
¼   teaspoon cayenne pepper
½   cup Chardonnay wine

Preheat oven to 350° F. Season chicken with salt and pepper. Set aside.

To make marinade, whisk together remaining ingredients. Pour half of the marinade on the chicken. Bake, covered, for 30 minutes.

Remove chicken from oven and pour remaining marinade over it. Return to oven and bake 20 to 30 minutes longer or until juices from chicken are clear.

Delicious served with rice.

Serves 4 to 6

Serve with Chardonnay.

Seafood

Broiled Salmon with Zucchini

2	tablespoons olive oil
¼	cup shallots, chopped
½	cup Chardonnay wine
1	cup cream or half and half
2	tablespoons lemon juice
4	salmon fillets
2	zucchini, sliced in thin lengthwise sections
¼	cup fresh dill, chopped
½	teaspoon sea salt or kosher salt
½	teaspoon black pepper
	Lemon and fresh dill for garnish

In a large skillet, heat one tablespoon of the olive oil and sauté shallots until golden. Add the Chardonnay and bring to a boil. After boiling about 1 minute, blend in the cream and lemon juice, and boil until the sauce is reduced to about 1 cup. Stir in dill, salt and pepper. Set aside and keep warm.

Brush salmon with remaining olive oil and broil until just cooked through on each side (3 to 5 minutes per side). While the salmon is broiling, steam zucchini sections until crisp-tender; drain.

To serve, place a bed of zucchini sections, topped with a salmon fillet, on each plate. Spoon warm cream sauce over each fillet. Garnish with a twist of lemon and a sprig of fresh dill. Excellent with wild rice.

Serves 4

Serve with Chardonnay.

Tomato-Crabmeat Vermicelli

1	tablespoon olive oil
1	large white onion, chopped
4	stalks celery, chopped fine
3	tablespoons chopped fresh parsley
1	clove garlic, minced
1	tablespoon chopped fresh basil
1	tablespoon chopped fresh oregano
2	large, fresh tomatoes, chopped
1	16-ounce can tomato paste
½	cup water
1	cup Chardonnay wine
1	pound crabmeat, chopped
½	pound vermicelli pasta
1	cup grated Parmesan cheese

In a large skillet, heat olive oil to medium-hot. Sauté onion and celery until soft and slightly brown. Add parsley, garlic, herbs, tomatoes, tomato paste, water and Chardonnay wine. Simmer for 30 minutes. Add crabmeat and heat.

Cook pasta according to package directions.

For each portion, serve pasta topped with crabmeat sauce and a generous sprinkling of cheese.

Serves 6

Serve with Chardonnay.

Two-Cheese Shrimp Casserole

2		medium onions, sliced
2		large tomatoes, sliced
1		pound shrimp, cooked and peeled

SAUCE	2	tablespoons butter
	2	tablespoons flour
	¼	teaspoon sea salt or kosher salt
	¼	teaspoon white pepper
	1	cup milk
	¾	cup medium cheddar cheese, cubed
	¼	cup Chardonnay wine
	1	6-ounce package provolone cheese, sliced
	2	slices white bread, crumbled

Preheat oven to 350° F.

In a small pan of water, boil onions gently over medium-high heat for 5 minutes. Place in the bottom of an 8 x 8-inch casserole dish. Layer tomato slices over onions and add shrimp.

To prepare cheese sauce, melt butter in a medium sauce pan. Stir in flour, salt and pepper. Add milk slowly, stirring continuously, until sauce thickens. Add cheese and stir until melted. Stir in Chardonnay. Pour cheese sauce over shrimp.

Cover casserole with provolone cheese slices and top with bread crumbs. Cook for 40 minutes or until the bread crumbs are brown and sauce is bubbly.

Serves 4

Serve with Chardonnay.

Shrimp and Chicken with Brown Sauce

½   cube butter, melted
1   tablespoon fresh minced garlic
2   cups onions, diced
2   cups mushrooms, sliced
1½ pounds chicken, boned and skinned
1½ pounds shrimp, peeled and deveined
1   teaspoon sea salt or kosher salt
½   teaspoon black pepper
½   cup Chardonnay wine
1   cup brown sauce (below)

SAUCE
¾   cup butter
¼   cup bacon drippings
1   cup celery, chopped
1   cup onion, chopped
½   cup carrots, chopped
1¼ cups flour

In a large skillet over medium heat, melt butter and sauté garlic, onions and mushrooms; set aside. Add chicken to skillet and sauté until almost done. Add shrimp, along with cooked garlic, onions and mushrooms; cook just until shrimp turns pink. Add salt, pepper, Chardonnay, and brown sauce; simmer briefly. Serve at once on cooked rice.

Brown Sauce: Sauté vegetables in butter and bacon drippings until tender. Stir in flour until smooth. Cook on medium heat until flour browns, about 10 minutes.

Serves 8 to 10

Serve with Chardonnay.

Trout Stuffed with Shrimp and Crab

¼ pound butter
1   tablespoon soy sauce
½   cup Chardonnay wine
2   tablespoons lemon juice
2   tablespoons celery, finely diced
2   tablespoons finely diced green onion
2   tablespoons finely diced green bell pepper
3   pounds small whole shrimp
3   pounds crabmeat, finely chopped
2   cups cooked brown rice
2   teaspoons lemon pepper
1   cup flour
6   8-ounce trout, boned, scaled, and fins removed
6   slices bacon, cooked and drained
    Parsley and lemon slices for garnish

In a large skillet over medium-low heat, melt 2 tablespoons of the butter. Add soy sauce, Chardonnay, lemon juice, vegetables, and seafood; sauté until vegetables are crisp-tender. Add cooked rice and continue cooking over low heat, stirring frequently.

Mix lemon pepper with flour and dredge trout in this mixture. In another large skillet, melt the remaining butter and sauté fish until done, about 3 minutes per side. Place trout on individual serving plates and stuff with seafood-rice mixture. Place a slice of fried bacon on top. Garnish with parsley and lemon.

Serves 6

Serve with Chardonnay.

Chardonnay Seafood Medley

1	tablespoon butter (softened)
2	tablespoons flour
1	cup water
4	scallops
16	prawns, shelled and deveined
2	tablespoons chopped shallots
1	tablespoon olive oil
1	cup Chardonnay wine
3	tablespoons fresh lemon juice
4	tablespoons whipping cream
½	teaspoon each kosher salt and white pepper
1	8-ounce package egg noodles, cooked
	Zest of 1 lemon for garnish
1	tablespoon fresh ground black pepper for garnish
2	scallions, thinly sliced, for garnish

Cream together butter and flour; set aside. In a medium saucepan, salt the cup of water and bring to a boil. Poach the scallops 1 minute and add prawns; poach 1 minute more. Remove seafood and reserve poaching liquid.

Sauté shallots in olive oil, add Chardonnay and reduce liquid by half. Add poaching liquid and lemon juice; bring to boil. Add butter and flour mixture and whisk until smooth. Simmer for 2 minutes; add cream; salt and pepper to taste.

Serve scallops and shrimp over noodles with lemon cream sauce. Garnish with lemon zest, black pepper and sliced scallions.

Serves 4

Serve with Chardonnay.

Basil Shrimp with Creme Fraiche

This delicious dish is easy to make, but the creme fraiche must be made two days before you cook the shrimp.

CREME FRAICHE (Requires 48 hours to mature)
1   cup heavy cream or whipping cream
1   cup dairy sour cream

¼   cup olive oil
1¾ pounds shrimp, peeled
1   teaspoon sea salt or kosher salt
½   teaspoon black pepper
2   cloves garlic, minced
2   cups fresh or frozen baby peas
½   cup Chardonnay wine
¾   cup creme fraiche
¾   cup fresh basil leaves, cut into narrow strips
1   package bow-tie or rotini pasta, cooked

NOTE: Prepare creme fraiche at least 2 days ahead.
To make creme fraiche, whisk heavy cream and sour cream together until thoroughly blended. Pour into a jar, cover and let stand in a warm place until thickened, about 12 hours. Stir well, cover, and refrigerate for 36 hours before using.

Heat olive oil in a large skillet over medium-high heat. Sauté shrimp just until pink. Add salt and pepper. Lower heat; add garlic, peas, and Chardonnay. Cook for 1 minute. Add creme fraiche and basil and cook another 1 to 2 minutes. Pour over pasta. Garnish with sprigs of fresh basil.

Serves 4

Serve with Chardonnay.

Shrimp and Crab with Feta-Tomato Sauce

2   tablespoons butter
1   clove garlic, minced
½   cup onion, finely chopped
1   tablespoon Dijon-style mustard
½   teaspoon dried tarragon leaves
4   medium tomatoes, peeled, seeded and chopped
½   cup Chardonnay wine
½   teaspoon sea salt or kosher salt
½   teaspoon black pepper
4   ounces feta cheese
½   pound raw shrimp, peeled and deveined
½   pound crabmeat
    Fresh parsley for garnish

In a large skillet over medium-high heat, melt butter. Stir in garlic, onion, mustard, and tarragon, and sauté for 5 minutes. Add tomatoes, Chardonnay wine, salt and pepper. Reduce heat and simmer for 10 to 15 minutes, stirring frequently, until sauce has thickened. Add feta cheese and simmer 10 minutes more.

Just before serving, add shrimp and crab and cook over low heat just until shrimp are pink. Garnish with parsley.

Serve over noodles or rice.

Serves 4

Serve with Chardonnay.

Spicy Shrimp and Potatoes

1	pound spinach, washed
¼	cup peach preserves
¼	cup Chardonnay wine
2	tablespoons lemon juice
2	teaspoons soy sauce
5	(about 1½ pounds) medium red potatoes, unpeeled
1	bunch (6 or 7) green onions, finely chopped
2	teaspoons all-purpose flour
1½	teaspoons paprika
1	teaspoon sea salt or kosher salt
1	teaspoon curry powder
2	tablespoons olive oil
1½	pounds large shrimp, shelled and deveined

Into a medium bowl, tear spinach into bite-sized pieces; refrigerate. In a small bowl, stir together peach preserves, Chardonnay, lemon juice, and soy sauce; set aside.

Cut potatoes into 1½-inch cubes. Cover with water in a 2-quart saucepan and bring to a boil; reduce heat, cover, and simmer 10 minutes or until potatoes are crisp-tender. Drain and place in a large bowl. In a small bowl, combine flour, paprika, salt and curry powder; pour half over potatoes and toss to coat. Pour remaining flour mixture over shrimp and toss to coat.

In a large skillet, heat olive oil to medium-hot; sauté potatoes and green onions, stirring occasionally, until vegetables begin to brown. Add shrimp to skillet and cook briefly, about 5 minutes. To serve, toss spinach with peach-preserves mixture. Arrange on a large platter with shrimp-and-potato mixture.

Serves 4 to 6

Serve with Chardonnay.

Sole au Gratin

4	tablespoons butter
4	sole fillets
¼	cup fresh basil leaves, loosely packed
4	fresh mint leaves
¼	pound mushrooms, sliced
	Juice of one lemon
½	teaspoon sea salt or kosher salt
½	teaspoon black pepper
½	cup Chardonnay wine
1	cup water
3½	tablespoons flour
1	cup grated cheddar cheese

In a large skillet over medium heat, melt 1 tablespoon of the butter. Add fish, basil, mint, mushrooms, lemon juice, salt and pepper. Add Chardonnay and water. Cover skillet and bring to a boil. When it reaches the boiling point, remove skillet from heat, turn fillets over, re-cover the pan, and let stand for 1 minute. Transfer fish to an ovenproof casserole; set aside. Return skillet to stove over medium heat and cook liquid with mushrooms for 2 or 3 minutes. Set aside.

In a medium saucepan over medium heat, melt the 3 remaining tablespoons butter. Add flour and cook 1 minute, stirring continuously. Add liquid with mushrooms from skillet; stir, and adjust seasonings. Reduce heat to low and cook sauce for 6 to 8 minutes. Pour over fish and sprinkle with cheese. Broil in the oven until cheese melts.

Serves 4

Serve with Chardonnay.

Seafood St. Jacques

1	pound scallops
½	cup sliced mushrooms
1	cup dry Chardonnay wine
1	small yellow onion, sliced
1	tablespoon chopped fresh parsley
2	teaspoons lemon juice
1	teaspoon sea salt or kosher salt
4	tablespoons butter
6	tablespoons flour
1	cup half-and-half
4	tablespoons shredded Gruyere cheese
¼	pound cooked crabmeat, shredded
½	pound cooked shrimp, peeled and deveined
	Bread crumbs
	Paprika

In a large skillet over medium heat, combine scallops, mushrooms, wine, onion, parsley, lemon juice and salt. Bring to a boil; simmer for 5 minutes. Drain, reserving 1 cup of the liquid.

In a medium saucepan over medium heat, melt the butter and stir in flour. Add cream and scallop liquid all at once. Stir until mixture thickens, then add cheese until it melts.

Add scallops, crabmeat and shrimp. Mix well and divide into 6 individual casseroles. Sprinkle with bread crumbs and paprika. Before serving, broil for 1 minute, or until mixture is bubbly.

Serves 6

Serve with Chardonnay.

Scallops in Saffron Chardonnay Sauce

3   tablespoons finely chopped shallots
2   tablespoons unsalted butter
1½   cups fish stock
1   cup Chardonnay wine
1   cup heavy cream
½   teaspoon saffron threads, crumbled
½   large orange: zest and juice
        Small pinch dried red chili pepper flakes
½   teaspoon sea salt or kosher salt
½   teaspoon white pepper
1½   pounds whole fresh sea scallops
4   tablespoons butter
        Fresh parsley for garnish

In a heavy saucepan over medium-high heat, melt butter and sauté shallots until translucent. Add fish stock and Chardonnay; boil until reduced by half. Add cream and reduce by half again, or until mixture coats back of spoon. Strain. Return to saucepan. Add saffron, orange zest and juice, red chili pepper flakes, and salt and pepper. Keep sauce warm. Makes about 1 cup.

Sauté scallops in melted butter for a few minutes, just until warmed through and opaque. Using a slotted spoon, divide scallops onto warmed serving plates and top with warm sauce. Garnish with parsley.

Serves 4

Serve with Chardonnay.

Desserts

Pear-Apricot Compote

2	large Bosc or other type pears, thinly sliced
4	large apricots, pitted and sliced
4	cinnamon sticks (about 1½-inches each)
4	teaspoons butter
6	tablespoons dried tart cranberries
½	teaspoon ground cloves
½	teaspoon ground nutmeg
½	teaspoon almond flavoring
1¼	cups Chardonnay wine
4	tablespoons light brown sugar
1	pound cake
½	cup broken walnuts (optional)
1	cup whipped cream (optional)
2	teaspoons finely shredded orange peel (optional)

In a large skillet over medium heat, melt butter and sauté pear and apricot slices with cinnamon sticks for 4 to 5 minutes. Add cranberries, cloves, nutmeg and almond flavoring. Cook for 3 minutes more.

Reduce heat. Add Chardonnay wine, brown sugar, and shredded orange peel. Simmer for 10 to 15 minutes, until pears are tender and cranberries soft. Remove and discard cinnamon sticks.

To serve, spoon fruit compote over pound cake. Garnish with whipped cream, broken walnuts or orange peel curls.

Serves 4

Serve with Chardonnay.

Italian Wine Sherbet

1   cup granulated sugar
1   cup water
1   teaspoon grated orange peel
1   teaspoon grated lemon peel
    Juice of 2 oranges
    Juice of 3 lemons
4   cups dry Chardonnay wine
    Meringue (recipe below)
    Jamaica rum (optional)
    Whipped cream and nut meats for garnish

MERINGUE
²/₃ cups granulated sugar
2   tablespoons water
¼   teaspoon vanilla extract
1   egg white, beaten stiff but not dry

In a medium saucepan, combine sugar and water; bring to a boil for 5 minutes. Remove from stove and cool. Place in ice-cream-freezer container, together with wine, grated lemon peel, grated orange peel, and orange and lemon juice. Freeze to soft-serve according to ice-cream freezer instructions.

(**NOTE:** If you do not have an ice-cream freezer, sherbet may be frozen in refrigerator trays. When mixture starts freezing around edges, transfer to chilled bowl, whip until smooth and replace in trays. Stir occasionally for smoother texture.)

Meanwhile, make meringue. Place sugar, water and vanilla in saucepan and cook until candy thermometer reads "soft ball"

or until a soft ball forms when a small amount of syrup is dropped into cold water. Pour sugar syrup gradually over egg whites, beating continuously. Cool.

When frozen sherbet reaches the soft-serve stage, blend in meringue and continue freezing for at least 2 more hours before serving.

To serve, sprinkle with rum, if desired, whipped cream, and nut meats.

Makes about 2 quarts.

Serve with Chardonnay.

Hot Cider Floats

Serve this simple, sweet treat after dinner in lieu of dessert.

4   **cups apple cider, heated to boiling point**
3   **teaspoons Chardonnay wine**
1½ **cups whipped cream**
6   **cinnamon sticks**
      Ground cinnamon for garnish

Pour hot apple cider into 6 demitasse cups. Stir ½ teaspoon Chardonnay into each cup. Carefully float a heaping spoonful of whipped cream on top. Place a cinnamon stick in each cup and add a dash of cinnamon.

Serves 6

Red, White & Blue Berry Dessert

3	tablespoons granulated sugar
½	teaspoon nutmeg
1½	cups fresh sliced strawberries
1½	cups fresh blueberries
½	cup Chardonnay wine, chilled
1	cup whipped cream
½	cup finely chopped almonds
4	maraschino cherries for garnish

In a small mixing bowl, stir together sugar and nutmeg; sprinkle over berries and stir gently. Refrigerate, and let stand for 2 hours.

Serve berries in individual chilled dessert dishes, topped with chilled Chardonnay, whipped cream, a sprinkle of almonds, and a maraschino cherry.

Serves 4

Serve with Chardonnay.

Sweet Potatoes and Apples Cake

½   **cup granulated sugar**
½   **teaspoon cinnamon**
1   **teaspoon nutmeg**
2   **pounds sweet potatoes**
¼   **teaspoon salt**
3   **apples, peeled, cored and sliced**
2   **tablespoons melted butter**
½   **cup orange juice**
½   **cup Chardonnay wine**
1   **teaspoon finely shredded orange peel**
½   **cup chopped walnuts**

Preheat oven to 325° F. In small bowl, combine sugar, cinnamon and nutmeg; set aside.

Cook sweet potatoes in salted water for 20 minutes or until tender. Drain, cool and peel. Cut into ½-inch slices and, alternating with layers of apples, arrange in a 9 x 12-inch buttered baking dish. Sprinkle each layer with sugar, nutmeg and cinnamon mixture. Pour butter and orange juice over all and bake for 30 minutes.

To serve, sprinkle with Chardonnay wine and garnish with shredded orange peel and chopped walnuts.

Serves 6

Serve with Chardonnay.

Broiled Peaches Chardonnay

1 can (1 lb. 13 oz.) peach halves in heavy syrup;
   reserve syrup
½ cup brown sugar
3 tablespoons butter
¼ teaspoon allspice
¼ teaspoon mace
1 teaspoon lemon juice
½ cup Chardonnay wine
   Vanilla ice cream

Arrange peach halves, hollow side up, in shallow baking dish; pour 1 cup of the reserved syrup over them.

Combine brown sugar, butter, allspice, mace, and lemon juice. Fill each peach half with brown sugar mixture, using all the mixture. Drizzle each filled peach half with 2 teaspoons Chardonnay. Broil 6 inches from heat for 5 minutes.

Serve hot (1 peach half per serving), topped with ice cream.

Serves 6 to 8

Serve with Chardonnay.

Chardonnay Custard

For added elegance, serve this dessert in stemmed glasses on pretty dessert plates.

4   **egg yolks**
4   **tablespoons granulated sugar**
     Dash of salt
½   **teaspoon lemon zest**
6   **tablespoons Chardonnay wine**
½   **cup whipped cream for garnish**

In the top of a double boiler over medium-high heat, combine egg yolks, sugar, salt and lemon zest. Beat with a wire whisk over hot (<u>not boiling</u>) water. (**NOTE:** Water should not touch upper pot.) Gradually add Chardonnay to egg-yolk mixture, beating continuously, until custard is fluffy-smooth and slightly thickened. Serve at once, or chill and serve later.

NOTE: Custard separates when cold. If this happens, stir it smooth again before serving.

Top custard with dollops of whipped cream. Excellent with crisp vanilla cookies.

Serves 4

Serve with Chardonnay.

Chardonnay Orange Mold

¾   cup granulated sugar
1   3-ounce package unflavored gelatin
1   cup Chardonnay wine
1   6-ounce can frozen orange juice concentrate
2   cups water
2   tablespoons lemon juice
    Dash of salt
    Zest of 1 lemon
2   cups heavy cream, whipped
1   11-ounce can mandarin oranges, drained
    Mint leaves for garnish

In a 3-quart saucepan mix sugar and gelatin. Stir in Chardonnay, orange juice concentrate, water, lemon juice, and a dash of salt. Heat to boiling, stirring continuously; boil for 1 minute. Remove from heat. Stir in lemon zest. Refrigerate until mixture mounds slightly when dropped from spoon, about 2½ hours.

Fold chilled gelatin mixture into whipped cream. Pour into a 7-cup mold. Refrigerate until firm, about 12 hours.

To serve, unmold and garnish with mandarin orange slices and mint leaves.

Serves 12

Serve with Chardonnay.

Figs in Honey and Chardonnay

½   cup honey
1   bottle Chardonnay
2   teaspoons grated lemon peel
2   tablespoons fresh lemon juice
¼   cup finely chopped fresh basil
¼   cup finely chopped fresh thyme
2½ pounds fresh figs
    Whipped cream or creme fraiche (see recipe pg. 69)
    Basil or thyme sprigs for garnish

In a large, nonreactive saucepan over medium-high heat, combine honey and Chardonnay; bring to a boil. Lower heat and cook, stirring continuously, until honey is completely dissolved. Add lemon peel, lemon juice, basil and thyme; stir. Place figs in Chardonnay syrup and poach over low heat, uncovered, for 4 minutes, turning figs every minute. Remove figs with slotted spoon and place in a large ceramic bowl. Continue cooking Chardonnay syrup until it is reduced to about 1 to 1½ cups.

At least 2 hours before serving, ladle some of the Chardonnay syrup into individual dessert bowls, add figs and chill.

To serve, top figs with whipped cream or creme fraiche. Garnish with basil or thyme sprigs.

Serves 4

Serve with Chardonnay.

Fresh Melons in Chardonnay Syrup

2   **cups late harvest Chardonnay**
1½ **tablespoons honey**
4   **¼-inch slices fresh ginger**
½   **teaspoon mace**
½   **vanilla bean**
5   **pounds assorted summer melons (pick your favorites**
     — heart of watermelon, cantaloupe, honeydew,
     crenshaw, casaba, or others)
     Mint leaves for garnish

In a large, nonreactive saucepan over high heat, combine Chardonnay, honey, ginger and mace. Split vanilla bean in half lengthwise; scrape seeds from pod; add seeds and pod halves to pan. Bring to a boil. Reduce heat to low and simmer, uncovered, for 5 minutes. Remove from heat. Discard vanilla pods and ginger slices. Set Chardonnay syrup aside to cool.

Meanwhile, cut melons in half. Scoop out seeds and discard. Using a melon baller, scoop out balls of the melon flesh and place them in a large ceramic bowl. Remove any remaining seeds and discard. Pour the cooled Chardonnay syrup over the melon, cover and chill for 1 hour or longer.

To serve, divide melon evenly among chilled individual bowls, spooning Chardonnay syrup over melon. Garnish with mint leaves.

Serves 6

Serve with Chardonnay.

Baked Banana Dessert

3	bananas, ripe but firm
½	cup orange juice
½	cup Chardonnay wine
¼	cup brown sugar, firmly packed
½	teaspoon cinnamon
½	teaspoon nutmeg
¼	cup grated coconut
3	tablespoons butter
½	cup heavy cream, whipped

Preheat oven to 350° F.

Peel bananas, slice lengthwise, and arrange cut-side down in a 9 x 13-inch glass baking dish. Pour orange juice and Chardonnay over bananas and sprinkle with the brown sugar, cinnamon, nutmeg and coconut. Dot with butter and bake for 20 minutes.

Serve with whipped cream.

Serves 6

Serve with Chardonnay.

Glossary and Pronunciation Guide

Al dente (al DEN-tee; al-DEN-tay): An Italian term for pasta that is cooked until tender but not soft, having a firmness that is somewhat resistant to the teeth. Literally, "to the tooth" in Italian.

Angel hair: Pasta cut into thin, extremely long strands.

Asiago (Ah-see-AH-go): A yellow cheese suitable for grating when aged, from Asiago, Italy.

Au Gratin (oh GRAHT-n): Food cooked with a top crust of bread crumbs and butter, sauce or grated cheese, and then browned in an oven.

Au Jus (oh ZHOOS): Meat served with its own natural juices from cooking.

Basil (BAYZ-l): A sweet, aromatic herb in the mint family which is cultivated for its leaves. When purchased fresh and not used immediately, basil will maintain its quality longer if it is placed in a container of water, stem ends down like a bouquet, and kept in the refrigerator. Basil is a main ingredient in pesto and is a popular seasoning in many modern recipes.

To baste (BAY-st): The process of spooning melted butter, hot fat, a sauce, or other liquid over meat as it roasts to keep it moist and juicy.

Bay leaf: The dried, aromatic leaf of the laurel or bay tree. It is normally used in a dried state as a flavoring for soups, stews, meats and other dishes, generally removed from the food prior to serving.

To beat: To stir rapidly with a circular motion, using a spoon, whisk, rotary beater or electric mixer, to give lightness to a mixture. Approximately 100 strokes by hand equals 1 minute by electric mixer.

Bisque (BISK): A rich, creamy soup made from fish, shellfish, meat, or puréed vegetables.

To blend: To stir a mixture until the ingredients are completely combined and smooth.

To boil: To immerse food in water, stock or other liquid when it has reached 212° F and is bubbling vigorously.

Bolognese (BO-la-neez): Characteristic of cuisine originating in the town of Bologna, Italy.

Bouillon (BOOL-yon; BOO-yon): A clear, thin broth generally made by simmering beef, chicken or vegetables with seasonings.

Bouillon (BOOL-yon) cube: A small cube of evaporated seasoned meat, poultry or vegetable stock used to make broth or add flavor to soups, stews and other dishes. Bouillon cubes are packed in small containers and sold in grocery stores.

Bouquet garni (boh-kay gar-nee): A bunch of herbs (traditionally 2 or 3 stalks of parsley, a sprig of thyme, and a bay leaf) tied together with string, wrapped in cheesecloth, or enclosed in a small cloth sack, then immersed in soups and stews to add flavor. The bouquet is removed from the cooked food before serving.

Caper (KAY-per): A pickled flower bud of the caper bush. Packed in salt or vinegar and sold in grocery stores, the pungent condiment is used in sauces, relishes, and many other dishes.

Casserole (KAS-eh-rohl): A dish, usually of earthenware or glass, in which food is baked and served. Both the container and the food prepared in it are referred to as a casserole.

Ceci (CHEH-chee): The Italian word for chickpea.

Chardonnay (shar-dn-AY; shar-doh-NAY): Currently, the most popular white wine grape worldwide.

Chervil (CHUR-vl): A delicate fernlike herb often used to flavor sauces and vinegars (often in combination with tarragon) and as a garnish. A member of the parsley family, chervil leaves are sweeter and more aromatic than standard parsley.

Chipotle (chih-POHT-lay): A dried, smoked jalapeño chili pepper, frequently canned in adobo sauce.

Chives (ch-eye-vs): The leaves of a bulbous herb of the lily family used as seasoning.

Chowder: A thick soup containing fish or shellfish and vegetables in a milk or tomato base. Or, a soup similar to this seafood dish.

Coquilles St. Jacques: (koh-KEEL sahn-ZHAHK, koh-KEE sahn-ZHAHK): A classic dish consisting of scallops in a creamy wine sauce, topped with bread crumbs or cheese and browned under a broiler, typically served in a scallop shell.

Cornstarch: A very fine flour made from corn, largely used as a thickening agent. To thicken a sauce, or gravy in a stew or casserole, make a little paste of cornstarch and water, stir this paste into the boiling liquid of the food you are cooking, and continue cooking and stirring until the sauce thickens.

Creme Fraische (krehm FRESH): A mixture of sour cream, powdered sugar, whipping cream, or other ingredients that has been allowed to ferment slightly, often used as a dessert topping or an ingredient in sauces. Literally, "fresh cream" in French.

Crisp-tender: Vegetables that are cooked until they are tender but not soft, having a fresh crispness that is somewhat resistent to the teeth.

Croissant (krwa-SAN; kre-SANT): A rich, crescent-shaped roll of leavened dough and puff pastry. Literally, "crescent" in French.

Curry powder: A pungent seasoning blended from chili, cinnamon, cumin, coriander, ginger, mustard, pepper, turmeric, and other spices. Curry powders are available from mild to hot depending on the amount of hotter spices used in the blend.

Deglaze (dee-GLAYZ): To dissolve the remaining bits of sauteed meat or roasted food and congealed juices from the bottom of a pan by adding a liquid and heating. First, the food is removed and excess fat discarded, then the remaining sediments are heated with stock, wine, or other liquid to make a gravy or sauce.

Dijon (dee-ZHON): A French city noted for its foodstuffs, including mustard.

Dijonnaise (dee-zhon-AZE): Characteristic of cuisine originating in Dijon, France, or foods containing Dijon mustard.

Dollop (DOLL-ehp): A small quantity or splash of a food substance.

Dredge (DREJ): To coat food by sprinkling it with flour, sugar, bread crumbs, or other powdery mixture or substance.

Farfalle; farfallini; farfallone (fahr-FAH-lay): Pasta shaped like small bow ties or butterflies. *Farfallini* are the smallest butterflies; *farfallone*, the largest.

Feta (FEHT-ah): A semisoft white cheese usually made from goat's or ewe's milk and often preserved in brine, which gives it a slightly astringent and salty flavor. From the modern Greek *pheta*, "slice of cheese"; and the Italian *fetta*, "slice".

Fennel (FEN-l): A Eurasian plant and its edible seeds or stalks. The edible parts have a pleasant anise flavor and are used to season foods.

Fettucine (FET-eh-CHEE-nee) : Pasta cut into narrow flat strips, or a dish made with this pasta.

Fideos (fih-DAY-ohs): Very thin vermicelli-type noodles.

Fines herbes (feen ZEHRB, feen ehrb) : A classic blend of finely chopped herbs, specifically chervil, chives, parsley, tarragon, and thyme, mixed together and used as a seasoning. Literally, "fine herbs" in French.

Florentine (FLOR-en-teen): Dishes that are prepared, cooked, or served with spinach, influenced by cuisine in Florence, Italy.

To garnish: To decorate prepared foods or beverages with small, colorful or savory items such as parsley, chopped scallions, flowers, mint leaves, or nuts.

Gnocchi (NYO-kee): Italian dumplings/pasta made of flour, corn meal, semolina, or potatoes, then poached or baked, and served with grated cheese and butter or a sauce.

Goulash (GOO-lahsh): A Hungarian stew of beef or veal and vegetables, seasoned mainly with paprika.

Green onion/scallion: An immature onion harvested before the bulb has developed. Both the green stem and the immature white bulb are delicious and can be used in recipes.

Gruyères (groo-YEHR): A nutty, pale yellow, firm cheese made from cow's milk, named for its area of origin in Switzerland .

Italian (ih-tal-yen): From or characteristic of Italy. The "I" in "Italian" is pronounced like the "I" in "Italy" (IH-tal-ee).

Jalapeño (ha-la-PEN-yo): A spicy red or green pepper.

Kale: A member of the mustard family with a slightly peppery flavor, usually green with large open leaves, .

Kosher salt: A refined, coarse-grained salt that has no additives.

Leek: A plant related to the onion.

Linguine/linguini (lin-GWEE-nee): Pasta cut into long, flat, thin strands.

Mace (may-s): An aromatic spice derived from the dried, lacy, outer coating of the nutmeg kernel. Mace and nutmeg can be used interchangeably.

Maraschino (mar-ah-SKEE-no) cherries: Sweet pitted cherries that are tinted with red food coloring and preserved in a sugar syrup. The name is derived from the Italian marasca cherry and the maraschino cordial made from the cherry's fermented juice and crushed pits.

Marjoram (MAR-jer-em): A spicy aromatic herb whose leaves are used for seasoning, especially popular in bread stuffing and with lamb.

Marinade (MARE-eh-nayd): A liquid combination, usually vinegar or wine, oil, and various herbs and spices, in which meat or vegetables are soaked before cooking.

Meringue (meh-RANG): A light, airy topping made of egg whites and sugar that is beaten until stiff, spread on pastry or pies, and baked until brown.

Milanaise (Mill-eh-neez): Food characterized by the style of cuisine in Milan, Italy, often containing macaroni, cheese, tomato and ham.

Mozzarella (mot-seh-REL-eh): A mild, white Italian cheese with a rubbery texture, often eaten melted on pizza and in Italian dishes. From the Italian *mozzare*, "to cut off".

Nutmeg: A sweet, nutty spice derived from the seed of the East Indies nutmeg tree. Grated or ground, nutmeg is popularly used in cakes, cookies, custards and white sauces.

Osso buco (oh-so BOO-ko): An Italian dish made with braised slices of veal shank, generally cooked in white wine.

To pare: To remove a very thin layer from the outer covering or skin of fruits or vegetables with a knife or vegetable peeler.

Parmesan (PAR-meh-zahn): A hard, sharp, dry Italian cheese made from skim milk. Its dry texture is ideal for grating or as a garnish. Its origin is Parma, Italy.

Penne (PEN-ay): Italian pasta shaped into small, short tubes with diagonally cut ends.

Pesto (PES-toh): A tangy sauce made with fresh basil, garlic, pine nuts, olive oil, and grated Parmesan cheese, used on pasta, in soups or stews, and as a dip.

Pilaf (pih-LAHF; PEE-lahf): A steamed rice dish often made with meat, seafood or vegetables in a seasoned broth.

Pistou (pee-STOO): The French word for pesto.

Piquant (PEE-kehnt; pee-KAHNT): Tasting pleasantly spicy, pungent or tart. From the Old French *piquer*, "to prick".

To pit: To remove stones or seeds from fruit.

Pith: The white part of citrus fruit between the peel and the flesh. Often bitter, it should be removed when peeling fruit.

To poach: To cook gently in simmering liquid so that the cooked food retains its shape.

Polenta: A thick mush made of cornmeal boiled in water or stock.

Proscuitto (pro-SHOO-toh): An aged, dry, spicy Italian ham that is usually sliced thin and served without cooking.

Provolone (pro-veh-LO-nee): A hard Italian cheese, usually smoked. From the Italian *provola*, a type of cheese.

Purée (pyoo-RAY): Fruit, vegetables, meat or other food that is rubbed through a strainer, sieved, or blended in a food processor to a thick cream. The ingredients are usually precooked before puréeing.

Ragout (ra-GOO): A stew in which the meat is usually browned before stewing, made from pieces of meat or fish that are cooked slowly without thickening.

Ramekin (RAM-ih-kin): Small, heatproof containers shaped like miniature soufflé dishes, used for individual servings.

To reduce: To diminish the quantity and improve the quality of a sauce or other cooking liquid by gently boiling until it becomes thicker and the flavor more concentrated.

Rice Pilaf: See pilaf.

Ricotta (rih-KAHT-ah): A soft, bland, fresh cheese that resembles cottage cheese, popularly used in lasagne, canneloni, and other Italian dishes. From the Latin *rococta* and *recoquere*, "to cook again".

Rosemary: An aromatic evergreen shrub whose leaves are used for seasoning lamb, pork, and other dishes.

Rotini (roh-TEE-nee): Italian pasta that is shaped into short spaghetti spirals.

Rotelle (roh-TELL-ay): Small round pasta that resembles a wheel with spokes.

Roux (ROO): A fat-and-flour mixture which is cooked together and used to thicken sauces. There are three types of roux – white, blond and brown. White roux is not cooked after the flour is added, blond roux is cooked until straw-colored, and brown roux is cooked until it is a dark brown color.

Sauerbraten (SOUR-BRAHT-n): A pot roast marinated in vinegar, water, wine, and spices before being cooked to give it a distinctive sharp flavor. Literally, "sour roast" in German.

To sauté (saw-TAY): To fry foods lightly in fat in a shallow open pan. Also, sauté refers to any dish prepared in this manner.

Scallion/green onion: An immature onion harvested before the bulb has developed. Both the green stem and the immature white bulb are delicious and can be used in recipes.

Scallops: Small, white shellfish that grow in fan-shaped shells with a radiating fluted pattern. 1) **Bay scallops** have a sweet, nutlike flavor and are relatively scarce; 2) **sea scallops**, have a robust taste and are more widely available.

Sea salt: Salt produced by the evaporation of sea water and that contains sodium chloride and trace elements such as sulfur, magnesium, zinc, potassium, calcium, and iron, generally used in a coarse state.

Seasoning: Salt, pepper, herbs and other flavorings used in cooking. To "adjust" or "correct" seasoning is to taste the food near the end of the cooking period to see if more salt, pepper or other seasonings are needed, then to add more to suit your taste.

Shallot (SHALL-et): A type of onion whose mild-flavored bulb is used in soups, sauces, stews, and other dishes. Shallots grow like garlic in a cluster on a common vine.

Sherbet (SHUR-bit): Frozen dessert made primarily of fruit juice, sugar, and water but also containing milk, egg white, or gelatin.

Simmer: To cook liquid gently at about 195° F or remain just at or below the liquid's boiling point.

To steam: To cook food by placing it on a rack in a closed container and exposing the food to moist steam heat (pressurized water vapor), being careful to keep the food away from boiling water below it.

St. Jacques (Sahn-ZHAHK): Seafood prepared in a creamy wine sauce, topped with bread crumbs or cheese and browned under a broiler.

Stock: A broth made by simmering meat, bones, poultry, vegetables or fish for several hours, used as a base in preparing soup, stew, gravy, or sauces.

Stuffing, dressing: A mixture of savory ingredients, usually highly seasoned, used to fill cavities in fish, poultry, or meat, or cooked separately. Although the terms are often used interchangeably, more precisely, *stuffing* is cooked inside the meat, fish, or poultry; *dressing* is cooked in a dish or pan.

To tenderize: To break down tough meat fibers, usually by marinating or beating it with a mallet.

Thyme (TYME): Any of several aromatic herbs whose leaves are used in *bouquet garni* and as a seasoning in soups, vegetables, stews, poultry, and other dishes.

Tortellini (tor-tl-EE-nee): Pasta shaped into small rings, usually stuffed with meat or cheese and served in soup or with a sauce.

To truss: To secure the legs and wings of poultry or game with string or skewers before cooking, which helps hold stuffing inside, maintains the bird's shape, and makes carving easier.

Vermicelli (ver-mih-CHEHL-ee): Italian pasta shaped into very thin strands, similar to but thinner than regular spaghetti. Literally, "little worms" in Italian.

To whisk: To beat quickly with a light circular motion, using a hand-held metal whisk or rotary beater, or an electric mixer, to incorporate air (fluffiness) into eggs, cream or food mixtures.

White pepper: A less pungent pepper ground from peppercorns from which the outer black layer has been removed, popular for use in light-colored sauces and foods.

White sauce: A sauce made with butter, flour, and milk, cream, or stock, used as a base for other sauces.

Wine
> **appellation (ap-peh-LAY-shuhn):** A protected name under which a wine may be sold, indicating that grapes used are of a specific kind from a specific district.
> **aroma:** The smell or fragrance of the wine.
> **body:** The perception of texture or consistency of a wine in the mouth.
> **bouquet (boh-KAY):** A unique and complex fragrance that emerges when a wine is fermented and aged.
> **complexity:** A complex wine has myriad layers and nuances of bouquet and flavor.
> **dry:** Dry wine has very little or no sweetness. In a *fully dry* wine, all sugar has been converted to alcohol during fermentation. A *medium-dry* wine contains a small amount of sugar, and an *off-dry* wine has the barest hint of sweetness. A wine may be both dry and fruity.
> **estate bottled:** The winery either owns or controls the vineyard and is responsible for the growing of the grapes used in the wine.

finish; aftertaste: The flavor characteristics of a wine that remain in the mouth and nasal passages after a wine has been swallowed.

nose: A wine's scent or fragrance. "A good nose" means the wine has a fine bouquet and aroma.

sweet: Sweet wine may result naturally from the amount of sugar in the grapes at harvest, or sweetness may be supplemented by the wine maker.

texture: Wine that is perceived as intense and full-bodied, producing a dense impression on the palate that makes the wine seem almost thick.

varietal (vehr-EYE-ih-tl): A wine named for the grape from which it is made. Although one or more grape varieties may be used in making a varietal, by United States law, the wine must be blended from at least 75 percent of the named varietal.

vintage (VIHN-tihj): The year grapes were grown and harvested. In the United States, the wine label may list the vintage year if 95 percent of the wine comes from grapes harvested that year.

viticultural (VIHT-ih-kuhl-cher-uhl) area: A region where grapes are grown.

Worcestershire (WOOS-ter-sheer; WOOS-ter-sher): A rich-bodied, piquant sauce of soy, vinegar, and spices, originating in the borough of Worcester (WOO-ster), England.

Zest: The outermost part of a lemon, lime, orange or other citrus fruit, usually finely grated or shredded, used to add subtle flavor or fruity piquancy to dishes.

Zucchini (zoo-KEE-nee): A variety of elongated, dark green squash. From the Italian *zucca*, "gourd".

INDEX

☆ *Cooking With Wine*
by Virginia and Robert Hoffman

Eighty-six American winery chefs share 172 of their
best recipes for cooking with wine and pairing food
with wine in this excellent cookbook. Whether you
are a novice or an expert in the kitchen, you'll enjoy
these great recipes. But that's not all. You'll also
learn how cooking with wine can be good for your health! Included is
a glossary of American wines and suggested pairings of wine and
food. This bestselling cookbook is considered a classic.

ISBN 0-9629927-3-9, softcover, 206 pages   **$15.95**

☆ *The Great Little Food With Wine Cookbook*
by Virginia and Robert Hoffman

There's a lot of information in this cookbook! You'll
enjoy excellent recipes by some of America's finest
winery chefs, tips on how and where to buy wine,
guidelines for selecting wine in restaurants, helpful
hints on deciphering wine labels so you know what
you're buying, and how to select wines to go with your meals ... and the
wines are all American.

ISBN 0-9629927-0-4, softcover, 118 pages   **$7.95**

☆ *The California Wine Country Cookbook II*
by Virginia and Robert Hoffman

Here are 172 exciting recipes from the most creative chefs of the California wine country. Recipes for appetizers, soups, salads, pastas, meats, seafood, poultry, vegetables and desserts — each an exciting addition to your culinary repertoire. Some recipes are quite simple, easy and fast to prepare. Others require more time and effort. All are innovative and will bring the cuisine of the California Wine Country into your home.

ISBN 0-9629927-6-3, softcover, 208 pages   **$12.95**

☆ *The California Wine Country Herbs & Spices Cookbook, New Revised Edition*
by Virginia and Robert Hoffman

Herbs and spices are the theme of this collection of recipes by 96 of the foremost chefs in the California wine country. You'll enjoy 212 of the best recipes that made them world famous for their cuisine. You'll discover exciting new ways to use 37 herbs and spices, how to make your own spice mixes, and how to make herbed and spiced oils and vinegars.

ISBN 0-9629927-7-1, softcover, 240 pages   **$14.95**

☆ *Great Salsas!*
by Virginia and Robert Hoffman

This collection of 96 salsa recipes takes you from mild and mellow to very hot. Discover delicious recipes from Latin America, the Caribbean, Africa, the Far East, and the American Southwest. Each is simple and easy to make ... and guaranteed to tantalize your taste buds. Come with us on a culinary adventure using exotic but easy-to-find ingredients, and enjoy new and exciting flavors, aromas to make your mouth water, and excitement in every taste!

ISBN 1-893718-05-0, softcover, 96 pages   **$7.95**

☆ *The Great Turkey Cookbook*
by Virginia and Robert Hoffman

Discover turkey — delicious, versatile, economical, and loadead with health benefits. This collection of 385 recipes puts turkey on the table every day (not just holidays) with its excellent recipes. Appetizers, soups, salads, pastas, sandwiches, chile, fajitas, barbecues and more. Plus, each recipe has a complete nutritional analysis — calories, cholesterol, fat, sodium and protein. A Book-of-the-Month Club selection for two years, more than 100,000 copies have been purchased. Truly a classic cookbook.

ISBN 0-893718-11-5, softcover, 388 pages   **$19.95**

ISBN 0-917413-05-9   **CD-ROM**   **$14.95**

Turkey Cookbook & CD-ROM package   **$29.95**

☆ *The Great Chicken Cookbook*
by Virginia and Robert Hoffman

Chicken is America's favorite! It's tasty, nutritious, convenient and economical. This book contains more than 400 fabulous recipes with timesaving tips and money-saving suggestions for great-tasting leftovers. Quick and easy to prepare, chicken is the perfect choice for the beginning cook and the experienced chef. Each recipe includes complete nutritional analysis and calorie count per serving.

ISBN 0-89594-828-1, softcover, 400 pages   **$19.95**

☆ *The Wine-Lover's Holidays Cookbook*
by Virginia and Robert Hoffman

You'll enjoy happier holidays with this timesaving collection of menus, recipes and wine recommendations. There are 13 seasonal holiday menus, with recipes and suggested American wines to accompany them, for Thanksgiving, Christmas, Chanukah, Passover, Easter and the 4th of July. Each is easy to prepare and appropriate for the selected holiday. This charming book is a perfect gift or remembrance for any special occasion.

ISBN 1-893718-03-4, softcover, 144 pages   **$9.95**

☆ Pairing Wine With Food
by Virginia and Robert Hoffman

In this handy bestselling book, more than 500 foods are paired with American wines. You'll learn where and how to buy wine, how to select wine in a restaurant, and even the right wines to pair with fast- and takeout foods such as nachos, Kentucky Fried Chicken, and. pizza. In addition, there's a helpful guide to American wines, and even a Winespeak Dictionary. With this unique book, you'll discover everything you've always wanted to know about pairing wine with food ... and more.

ISBN 1-893718-01-8, softcover, 96 pages   **$8.95**

☆ Nancy's Candy Cookbook: How to Make Candy at Home the Easy Way
by Nancy Shipman

Have fun and save money by making top-quality candy at home. In this step-by-step guidebook, candy specialist Nancy Shipman takes you through the candy-making process and shares her favorite recipes — fudge, divinity, brittles and barks, caramels and nougats, nut clusters, chews, cream, fruit and nut centers, mints and jellies, lollipops, taffy, chocolate pizza, and many more. There are more than 100 excellent candy recipes plus helpful information on types of chocolate and other sweet ingredients, candy-making equipment, dipping and coating, and much more. You'll become an expert candy maker in no time. How sweet it is!

ISBN 1-877810-65-7, softcover, 192 pages   **$14.95**

☆ *Cooking with Chardonnay: 75 Sensational Chardonnay Recipes*

by Barbara and Norm Ray

NEW!

Chardonnay is one of the most popular white table wines worldwide. Its unique flavors are ideal for drinking and cooking, many excellent vintages are readily available at reasonable prices, and it pairs well with today's lighter cuisine. In this new cookbook you'll enjoy 75 sensational, easy-to-prepare recipes, each of which is flavored with Chardonnay — soups, pastas and grains, meats, poultry, seafood, and desserts. In addition, you'll appreciate the introduction to Chardonnay, helpful guides on how to cook with wine, decipher wine labels, and serve wine, a glossary and pronunciation guide for wine cooking terms ... and more.

ISBN 1-877810-54-1, softcover, 128 pages   **$9.95**

NEW!

☆ *Cooking with Merlot: 75 Marvelous Merlot Recipes*

by Barbara and Norm Ray

If you, your family, and friends enjoy moderately heavy cuisine with rich wine overtones, think Merlot! This exciting, new cookbook contains 75 marvelous, easy-to-prepare recipes, each of which is flavored with Merlot — soups, pastas and grains, meats, poultry, seafood, and desserts. In addition, there's an introduction to Merlot, helpful guides on how to cook with Merlot, decipher wine labels, and serve wine, a glossary and pronunciation guide for wine cooking terms ... and more.

ISBN 1-877810-53-3, softcover, 128 pages   **$9.95**

☆ ☆ ☆

ORDER

To order Hoffman Press cookbooks through the mail, please complete this order form and forward with check, money order or credit card information to Rayve Productions, POB 726, Windsor CA 95492. If paying with a credit card, you can call us toll-free at 800.852.4890 or fax this completed form to Rayve Productions at 707.838.2220.

We invite you to visit the Hoffman Press Website and view our cookbooks at foodandwinebooks.com.

☐ Please send me the following book(s):

Title _____ Price _____ Qty ___ Amount _____

Title _____ Price _____ Qty ___ Amount _____

Quantity Discount: 4 items@10%; **7 items@15%; 10 items@20%**	Subtotal $ _____
	Discount $ _____
	Subtotal $ _____
Sales Tax: Californians please add 7.5% sales tax	Sales Tax $ _____
Shipping & Handling:	
Book rate — $3 for first book + $1 each additional	Shipping $ _____
Priority — $5 for first book + $1 each additional	Total $ _____

Name _____ Phone _____

Address _____

City State Zip _____

☐Check enclosed $ _____   Date _____

☐Charge my Visa/MC/Discover/AMEX $ _____

Credit card # _____   Exp. _____

Signature _____ *Thank you!* _{wine402}